Fearless

In the Face Of...

Today

Mike Thornton

PH

P.H. Services, LLC
Colorado Springs, CO

P.H. Services, LLC
Colorado Springs, CO
phservices.books@gmail.com
www.needanewplan.com

ISBN: 9798986846637
Library of Congress Catalog No. In progress...

Cover Design by Mike Thornton
Editor: P.H. Services, LLC

To Linda,
The compass that keeps me on a true course

Titles By Date

Titles Alphabetically

Introduction

Are you tired of mediocrity in your Christian life? Are you done with society's moral decline in the name of "woke"? Are you looking for answers? In *Fearless*, you'll get the truth—God's Word—and the Rock upon which you can build your future. You'll be encouraged, strengthened, and pointed to the only source that IS truth—the Bible.

Over 100 times in Scripture, we're told "do not fear" or "do not be afraid." Because that is a prominent theme, it must be important to God. Why then, are so many living in fear? I believe that as a result, they've lost their peace. The world can be a scary place. How does one reacquire one's peace?

Aside from the common fears of spiders and public speaking, the fear of the unknown ranks high on many people's list. Why is that? The unknown spawns hopelessness when we don't know or forget who is in charge of the future. Today's world scene is definitely changing. Is it good change or just moral decline? Hmmm. For sure moral decline.

I agree there IS a systemic problem, but it's NOT racism or anti-semitism. It's an eye problem. As a society, we've lost our focus, forgotten why our forefathers left their homes for a better world. The tyranny of the English throne got to the breaking point and brave men and women said "enough." The freedom to practice religion as we choose was one of the driving forces behind the decision to get on the boats.

Some will say, "That was then, this is now. Times have changed." That's true. However, just because we're on a slippery slope—a societal moral decline that, with each increment of decline, comes the new normal—doesn't justify turning our backs on the One who, for two and a half centuries, has blessed our nation beyond any before. As morals and values have "left the building," so has peace. No longer do we look out for each other, our neighbors, or those who don't look, think, or believe as we do. But fear of just about everything has replaced caring for others with distrust, anger, and hatred.

Our systemic problem is also an "I" problem. WIIFM (what's in it for me) has pooh-poohed our communal value system and replaced it with a self-centered, me-at-all-costs mentality. Actions have consequences. Good actions—good consequences; bad actions—bad consequences.

We do have an enemy, but it's not our neighbor, not the illegal alien, and not those people who look and sound different than us. This enemy would not only harm us on earth, but his diabolical goal is to lie us into hell where the Bible says, *"In that place, there will be weeping and gnashing of teeth..." (Luke 13:28)*. He's the one fanning the flames of hatred, dissatisfaction, jealousy and more. All toward one end: to destroy you. *"The thief* [Satan] *comes only to steal and kill and destroy..."* (John 10:10)

This book is committed to one purpose, spreading the good news that **Jesus Christ came into the world to save sinners.** (I Tim. 1:15) And in that knowledge, hope is born. Jesus finished the verse above about the destroyer, by saying, *"...I came that they may have life, and have it abundantly."* Jesus' words are intended to nurture and solidify our hope. Hope in the right thing or person, knowing that world events haven't sneaked up on God and He's busy "recalculating," should not only return us to a peaceful state, but also fill us with joy and excitement that we'll soon be home in heaven with Jesus.

If you're not experiencing the abundant life that Jesus offers, and I don't define that as health and wealth but *"love, joy, peace patience, kindness, goodness, faithfulness, gentleness, self-control"* (Gal. 5:22, 23), don't wait to see how bad it's going to get. It will only get worse. And tomorrow is not promised to anyone.

I've been asked "Why do you write?" The only answer I had until today was, "Because I can't help it and I feel it's a calling." But now I have a different answer. I have prayed that God would take the words and ideas He's given me (no, I'm not claiming Divine Inspiration) and distribute them as He sees fit. Just now, I came across Habakkuk 2:2,3: *"Then the Lord answered me and said, 'record the vision and inscribe it on tablets, that the one who reads it may run. For the vision is yet for the appointed time; It hastens toward the goal and it will not fail. Though it tarries, wait for it; for it will certainly come, it will not delay.'"* I'm not predicting the future. It's already settled in heaven. I'm just drawing attention to what God said and warns us of. If one person is helped into or back to a saving relationship with Jesus Christ because of my writing, it will all have been worth it.

I believe we're seeing the end-time prophesies come to pass right before our own eyes. No, I'm not setting any dates. Only God knows the when of our call home. This book, and *Christ in Men…Today* are written to men especially, but apply to all who have breath, male and female. It is a call to arms, a wake-up call that our time is short. It is an encouragement to live what we say we believe, with no fear, because *"Greater is He who is in us than he who is in the world* (Jn. 4:4)."

Each writing in the book stands on its own. But you'll see a common thread spanning the entire book. It's because of my passion to elevate God's word to a position of prominence in our lives. A position that demands obedience and promises great rewards. I am saddened when I look at today's organized church. Many are going through the motions and it's questionable if they even know or have a personal relationship with Jesus Christ. I'm sad because the devil has lied and convinced them all that's required is church attendance, give a little each Sunday, then live the rest of the week with little to no discernible difference from the world.

Christmas is coming and the angel's announcement in Luke 2:14 of "peace on earth" doesn't mean some distant day we'll never see. It is available to everyone, now, if we meet the criterion of the rest of the verse: *"among people with whom He is pleased."* You want peace back? Is God pleased with you?

My prayer is that this book finds its target, the soul hungry for more. More than the world offers. More than pop psychology offers. More than fortune-cookie wisdom. Everything written points the reader to the only answer to any and all of the world's problems: Jesus Christ. *"The Lord takes pleasure in those who fear Him, in those who hope in His* mercy (Psa. 147:11)." Will you become *"Fearless in the Face of..."* with me?

July 28, 2020

Is it "customer service" or "customer serve us"?

Today, my rant will hopefully lead to a couple of godly truths that I need to hear. Y'all can look over my shoulder.

Recently I've dealt with my newspaper distributor and my cable company. Both have auto-attendants to answer their phones. If I wanted to yell at a computer, I have enough opportunity at my own desk; I don't need to sit in queue and listen to the same four bars of some techno "music" on top of it.

What ever happened to "the customer is always right?" And I didn't even have a complaint; just wanted to ask a clarifying question. Couldn't get past the electronic screener. Thought maybe I wasn't speaking loud enough. My wife came in and ask who I was yelling at. Never did get to a real person or get my question answered. But before I digress too far...

The Bible tells me to, *"consider it all joy my brethren when you encounter various trials."* (James 1:2) Well this was certainly a trial for my patience, tolerance, and yes, my joy. I guess my trial-ometer is reading in the red because I seem to be getting more of them. So, what's my takeaway? I'm no better than what I'm complaining about. If I really believe that God is in control of everything that happens to me—and I do—and allows things to polish my rough edges—and there are many—then life's hiccups shouldn't be a threat, a disruption of MY plan that can derail me.

My wife and I have a code, the number 413, that she can say when I'm on thin ice. It's to remind me that I'm not observing the challenge of Ephesians 4:1-3: *"walk worthy, with all humility, gentleness, patience, tolerance, unity, bond of peace"* so I don't crash through and have to be rescued.

You probably don't have any of those trials, or days where you need a reminder as I do occasionally. That's great. But just in case, why don't you memorize these three verses and keep them in your arsenal of weapons against him who would destroy us.

Until next time...

Aug 2, 2020

Is there really a God?

Living in Colorado, I am exposed to the beauty and majesty of God's creation daily. Whether I look at the sunrise or sunset, or the incredible 14ers (for you non-Coloradans, those are mountains that exceed 14,000 feet), one of which I see from my deck, or watch a lightning storm spread from mountain to plain, I'm reminded of Psalm 19:1-3, "*The heavens are telling of the glory of God, and their expanse is declaring the work of His hands. Day to day pours forth speech, and night to night reveals knowledge. There is no speech, nor are there words; their voice is not heard.*"

Romans 1:19, 20 gives us further proof, "*…because that which is known about God is evident within them; for God made it evident to them. For since the creation of the world His invisible attributes, His eternal power, and divine nature, have been clearly seen, being understood through what has been made, so that they are without excuse.*"

If you were in a courtroom, watching an important trial, and undeniable evidence like what we just read was presented, you'd have no choice but to go along with whichever side did that presentation. So why do men still deny there is a God? It's simple, really. Go back to Psalm 19, verse 1. "The heavens are telling…their expanse is declaring…no words…voice is not heard."

Just what is the story being told? In the silence of observation, that there IS a God. He's powerful. He's creative. But, to accept that as fact, one has to recognize that if there is a "creation" then there HAS to be a "Creator." Just like if there is a house, there had to be a contractor. Intelligent design, which is everywhere in nature, demands a designer. Stuff doesn't migrate from nothing to something, changing and adding along the way. Chaos never evolves to order, but the opposite is always true. Because man's pride (and sin) doesn't go quietly, he knows that if there really is a Creator, then he would be accountable to Him and He has the right to set the rules. That conclusion would mean giving up self-rule and we hate the thought of not being in control.

I believe the main reason for not flocking to God, aside from not giving up our pride, is that the big picture has not been effectively painted. Let me make it simple. There IS a God and He loves us. But He is righteous and doesn't tolerate sin. We sin. That separates us from God. The penalty? Death. Yes, there is a heaven and a hell. And we will spend eternity in one or the other. There's no third option. We have an enemy named Satan. He is a liar and clever. His pitch hasn't changed from the Garden of Eden. He lures us with lies about God, lies about what satisfies, and lies about our future.

Because of God's love for us, and His wanting us to spend eternity with Him, He sent His son, Jesus Christ, to earth to share God's message of love and forgiveness. His mission? To die in our place because we could never meet God's standard of holiness. We could never amass enough good deeds, give enough to worthy causes, or live a life without sin. Therefore, our destiny apart from Jesus Christ is eternity in hell. You think things are bad in the world now, just wait. In a short time, all the Christians in the world will be called to leave this world (it's called the Rapture) and meet Jesus to begin our new lives in eternity.

If you don't admit and get rid of your pride and recognize the truth of Christ's death, burial, and resurrection on your behalf, you'll be part of the crowd that finds out first-hand just how bad things can get…but only for three and a half years. Then bad becomes worst and there's no second chance, no excuses (see verse above).

Our Creator wants us to know Him, wants us with Him forever. That's why He gave us His Word that describes Him and His plan for us. Don't be one who falls for the devil's lies. The ONLY truth you can bet your future on is the Bible. Read it. Believe it. Turn to Jesus as your only hope. Time is short and there isn't anything prophesied with regard to "the end" that still needs to happen before Jesus calls us home. Get ready by confessing that you're a sinner and can't save yourself. Trust that Christ's death on the cross paid your tab. If you do that, your future in heaven is secure. Find a good Bible-believing church and get involved in corporate worship, fellowship, and some kind of ministry to share what has happened to you.

Aug 3, 2020

Good News Monday

While reading in Romans this morning, I came to chapter 8. I don't know how many times I've read this section, but instead of just cruising by (sometimes that happens with familiarity), verse 1 really jumped off the page at me. *"Therefore there is now no condemnation for those who are in Christ Jesus."* The thought struck me that with all the bad news day and night for the past 5 or 6 months, we could use some good news today. And what could be better news than this verse?

I'm sure at one time or another, we've all been sent to the principal's office, gotten spanked or a timeout from our parents, or gotten a speeding ticket. Chances are good we deserved every one of them. What if we had a friend who offered to take our punishment? Or a real-life get-out-of-jail-free card?

That's the reality, the truth, the good news of today's verse. No condemnation. Try to wrap your mind around that. No punishment, no jail time, no permanent record of wrongdoing. Not guilty. I'm in.

Further good news. It's available to anybody. But there is one prerequisite, the last part of the verse: *"...for those who are in Christ Jesus."* Doesn't seem like much of a requirement for all that we get in return. What's the catch? Only that we have to *be willing* to give up anything that resists putting Christ first in our life, to put to death our pride, and come on God's terms. Jesus said, *"I am the way and the truth and the life, no one comes to the Father but through me."* (John 14:6) Jesus is THE ONLY way to God. Not good deeds. Not large donations.

We tend to focus on what we have to give up rather than on what we get now and for eternity. We have a very near-term focus. Consider this. We may live 80 years on earth. The Bible says, *"For a thousand years in Your sight are like yesterday when it passes by, or as a watch in the night."* (Psalm 90:4) A watch is 4 hours. A day has 6 watches. If we do the math, 80 years on our calendar is like 175,000 years in heaven. And at that point, eternity is still running the opening credits. The movie hasn't even started.

Just as heaven is real, so is hell. It's described by Jesus as *"in that place, there will be weeping and gnashing of teeth."* (Matt. 25:30) Doesn't sound like a place I want to spend a minute let alone eternity.

Jesus said, *"...the one who comes to Me I will certainly not cast out."* (John 6:37) Don't be like the rich man in Jesus' parable who, when Jesus told him to sell everything and follow Me, *"went away grieving; for he was one who owned much property."* (Matt. 19:22)

There is nothing, let me say it again, nothing you possess, nothing on your agenda, nothing in your past, present, or future that you shouldn't be willing to shed in exchange for eternity with Jesus who IS the friend who took our punishment on the cross. Don't let it be in vain.

Now that's what I call good news. Stay tuned...

Aug 4, 2020

Anniversary of a Homegoing

Sixteen years ago today, God blew the whistle for my 27-year-old son Dan to get out of the pool. My wife and I were awakened by a 2:00 A.M. phone call with the news that Dan was gone. I use that word not because I'm afraid to say "dead" but because Dan isn't. He's in heaven with Jesus—very much alive, and at peace.

I think the best thing about knowing the Lord Jesus Christ is He is the source of hope. Hope for a future without death, in His presence, reunited with loved ones who knew Him before they died. And it's forever. Read yesterday's post for a peek into how long that is.

The Bible says, "...*in Your book were all written the days that were ordained for me, when as yet there was not one of them.*" (Psalm 139:16) We all have an expiration date. Thankfully, God doesn't let us know ahead of time when it is. But the other side of that is that we must be ready to go at any time. My wife and I have buried two children. Dan and his 1-year-old sister Staci 46 years ago.

As I mentioned yesterday, I'm reading in Romans. Today, chapter 14 was part of it. What an appropriate section to remind me of what my son is experiencing. "...*for the kingdom of God is not eating and drinking, but righteousness and peace and joy in the Holy Spirit.*" (Romans 14:17) I think of all the evil he has missed out on these past 16 years, especially the rampant hatred that is now expressing itself in riots, burning, and looting under the false flag of "black lives matter."

My hope—more than hope, a belief—is that soon I and all who love Jesus will be experiencing the righteousness, peace, and joy Paul talked about in Romans. Are you ready? I think I can hear the trumpet player warming up. Read I Thess. 4:16 to understand that reference.

Aug 10, 2020

Consistency

So I'm reading this morning about Paul and his defense of his consistency, of being the same person whether present or absent. False apostles had been trying to stir up the Corinthians against him by saying, "*'His letters are weighty and strong, but his personal presence is unimpressive and his speech contemptible (2 Cor. 10:10).*" And it got me thinking about consistency. It's one of the things we count on in life; we don't want products or people to change (other than to get better).

So how does that apply to our Christian walk? I've never really thought about how important consistency is in our faith with respect to what others observe in us. But today it struck me as *very* important.

Part of the history of the word "hypocrite" is "a pretender, to play a part on stage." We are new creatures in Christ, the old things passed away (II Cor. 5:17). So why do I sometimes still struggle with playing the part of my old self? It's because I'm a work in progress; theology calls it sanctification.

How does one attain consistency? It starts with an awareness of who's watching and a commitment to not play the chameleon. Actors have to please the director, the investors, and ultimately the audience. And we know they're just playing a part. As followers of Christ, our primary goal should be to please the audience of One. If we do that, others—and there are many—who may be watching will not see much, if any, difference between what we say (or write) and what we live out day to day.

We think of consistency as something stable, unchanging regardless of changes in circumstances. The irony for the Christian is that we should be constantly changing, *consistently* becoming more like Jesus each day. Let's face it, being a Christian isn't easy. Jesus said, "*In the world you have tribulation, but take courage, I have overcome the world.*" (John 16:33)

The world, our flesh, and the devil don't want us growing more like Christ. Temptation is all around. Idolatry is insidiously subtle and pulling us to go with the flow. The best thing we can do is keep our "sword" sharp. Spend time in God's Word daily. Find a kindred spirit to share the journey with. We're called the *family of God*. Families work and play *together*. King Solomon said, *"Two are better than one… for if either of them falls, the one will lift up his companion. But woe to the one who falls when there is not another to lift him up"* (Eccl. 4:9,10).

As you go through today ask yourself, "Am I consistent in my walk regardless of who's looking? Do I need someone to lift me up or is there someone who needs me to do the lifting?" And sticky-note the word "consistency" where you'll see it often.

Thanks for reading.

Aug 17, 2020

Justice—Be careful what you wish for.

Where does justice come from? Mom and dad? Your boss? The police? Courts? Congress? Maybe…a long time ago when society operated with a strong moral compass and had a sense of right and wrong: a higher standard most people agreed to and our country was founded upon. Today? Not so much.

We watch or read the news and see example after example where "justice"—at least our definition of it—goes unrequited. "Getting away with murder" is no longer a catch-all category for bad behavior; it literally means what it says. We feel cheated when we see the bad guys go free. Why?

God has placed within the heart of man an ability to discern right from wrong. Ignoring it doesn't make it go away, but it does deaden it. Over time, as we continued to accept lower standards, the envelope of acceptable behavior got stretched to the breaking point. We are now there. Look around at the disregard for law, the disrespect for authority, and the lack of accountability both intrinsic and enforced.

So what's ahead? Justice, perfect and swift, is on the horizon. But it may not be what you expect or even want…unless you know Jesus Christ as your Savior. Because of man's depravity apart from knowing and living for Jesus, it is pure folly to try and fix the world's system. But God's justice will be perfect. His standard is holiness, black and white (no gray area), we either meet it or we don't. Spoiler alert: we don't.

We have had millennia to learn to be "good enough." The Bible tells us how that's working out, *"The fool has said in his heart, 'There is no God.' They are corrupt, they have committed abominable deeds; there is no one who does good…not even one."* (Psalm 14:1,3) When judgment comes (read Revelation 6-19), it will be swift (7-year tribulation), terrible, and no one will escape.

The countdown clock is ticking. Jesus upbraided the Pharisees and Sadducees for their blindness, *"Do you know how to discern the appearance of the sky, but cannot discern the signs of the times.?"* (Matt. 16:3) That message is germane for us today. The signs that were foretold over 2,000 years ago are being fulfilled in our present day. If you're reading this, it's not too late. Jesus Christ is your ONLY solution and hope to escape the justice that is coming. Don't stop here. There is another side to this story. God IS righteous and WILL judge. But He does it because **HE LOVES YOU**. to see the rest of the story, go to Steps To Salvation in the appendix. *"The Lord is my portion, says my soul. Therefore I have hope in Him."* (Lamentations 3:24).

August 20, 2020

Is It Still 'Today'?

You can't sleep. You're anxious about tomorrow. Are you a little child waiting for Christmas morning? Or are you an adult living in 2020? They're both anticipating the unknown. So what makes the difference? One has hope, the other fear and pessimism. But it doesn't have to be that way. If you're in the latter category, you can have hope too. And the object of that hope is real and not just wishful thinking.

In Hebrews, we're told to *"encourage one another day after day as long as it is still called "Today," so that none of you will be hardened by the deceitfulness of sin"* (Heb. 3:13). You say, "What's encouraging about today?" And I understand that perspective, what with the media constantly reminding us to social distance and wear masks because we're spreading death everywhere we go.

HTTP://NeedANewPlan.com is in the business of GOOD NEWS. Today is no exception. We—those of us who know the Lord Jesus Christ as Savior—have a lot to be encouraged about.

At the top of the list is the fact that the God of the universe knows our name: *"**Do not fear**, for I have redeemed you; I have called you by name; **you are Mine**!"* (Isa. 43:1b, emphasis added). Next, we are His *because* we believe in God's son Jesus for the forgiveness of our sins. The list goes on and on. Permit a couple more. Our future is secure with Christ. The worst man can throw at us cannot cause God to lose His grip on us, *"...no one is able to snatch them out of the Father's hand"* (John 10:29). And one of the best, *"As far as the East is from the West, so far has He removed our transgressions from us"* (Psalm 103:12).

If that doesn't encourage us, either our faith is small or our (little 'g') god is small. Re-read my list, then develop one of your own. By the time you've got half a dozen items you're thankful for, you'll be like a little kid waiting for Christmas...only better because Heaven isn't just for a day.

August 23, 2020

The BIG Lie

Joe Biden isn't "The Father of Lies," neither is Chuck Schumer. But has it occurred to you that in our society lying is ubiquitous? It has gotten to the point of incredulity. Some are so blatantly false, yet repeatedly told with straight faces. It seems proof or scientific evidence to the contrary that pokes holes in the lie just isn't enough.

"The Big Lie" concept is said to have started with Adolph Hitler in *Mein Kampf* in 1925. Fifteen or sixteen years later, Joseph Goebbels, a radical German Nazi, is credited with the following from an article in January 1941, "*The essential English leadership secret does not depend on particular intelligence. Rather, it depends on a remarkably stupid thick-headedness. The English follow the principle that when one lies, one should lie big and stick to it. They keep up their lies even at the risk of looking ridiculous.*" Think of that in context of today's politics.

I just finished a 2008 novel by David Baldacci, *The Whole Truth*, in which (at the time) a relatively new business was flourishing; the business is PM or Perception Management. It's built on the concept that we can **create truth** to serve our purpose. And with a lazy and gullible population, fed by a lazy and partisan media, the bigger the lie, the more unbelievable, the more likely it'll go down without water.

The statement, "If a lie is big enough and told often enough, people will believe it" doesn't have an authenticated source. However, one only has to look at today's political dialog to see it in action and become confused by competing claims, especially about all the "science" behind masking up. You have to ask yourself, "What's the endgame and who benefits?"

I bore you with all this to set the stage to make my point. There IS a father of lies; his name is Satan (John 8:44). Why does he lie? Aside from the fact that it's his nature and he can't help it, he does it because he hates Jesus Christ and by extension, His followers. But there is one source of truth that is never wrong, never leads astray, and paints an amazing picture of hope—The Bible. Satan will try to convince you that the path to hell is labeled "heaven" and is filled with all the shiny objects one could want. Don't fall for it. The true path to heaven is clearly labeled "Jesus."

The acid test of a prophet is they have to be 100% correct 100% of the time. The penalty for missing the mark? Death. EVERY Old Testament prophet of God met the standard. How do we know? Because their prophecies were fulfilled to the letter in the New Testament. The ones that weren't, have future dates on them. So why do I mention that? To add credibility, assurance, and hope. If God's Word written by His prophets NEVER missed the mark—and there were hundreds of prophetic events—then it's a safe bet that those describing the future won't either. I use the word describing rather than predicting because to God who lives in eternity, the events have already happened.

We are living in a time when some of the unfulfilled prophecies are coming true. So what? you ask. Only that our world has an expiration date that could be closer than we think. When that happens, those of us who believe in the Lord Jesus Christ as our Savior will be snatched (raptured) from this planet to begin eternity in heaven with God our Father and His Son Jesus. Those who don't know Him will be left behind to endure seven years of worldwide chaos—the Bible calls it The Tribulation—after which all will be judged and found guilty. Hell awaits.

I pray all who are reading this will be in the first group. If you're not sure and would like to be, go to the Appendix "Steps To Salvation" for a step-by-step plan for you to understand your options.

August 24, 2020

How's Your Memory?

Our memories are funny. I can remember most of the words to oldies I hear on radio, but sometimes forget why I went into the garage. It's easy to get sidetracked if, on the way to do one thing, something else grabs my attention. Peter spoke to the issue of memory this morning in my reading. *"For he who lacks these qualities* [listed in v 5-7] *is blind or short-sighted, **having forgotten his purification from his former sins**."* (2 Pet. 1:9)

For those of us who have known Jesus for a while, it's easy to forget (or gloss over) the sins from which we've been delivered and take for granted our salvation in Christ. In Jesus' message to the churches in Revelation 1-3, He tells the church in Ephesus, *"Therefore remember from where you have fallen, and repent…"* (Rev. 2:5) In the Lord's Supper, we're told, *"…do this in remembrance of Me."* (Luke 22:19) What is it we're supposed to remember about Jesus? Our sins and the cost to Him personally to redeem us. Picture the agony of being nailed on a cross. Then remember that YOU and I put Him there.

Throughout our day, things pull at us from all directions. We're busy. We're tired. Ask yourself, "Today, am I thankful for what Jesus did FOR ME?" Hopefully, you can say yes. The best way to show Him our thanks is to live each day in humility and gratitude.

Today, make a commitment to start every day by thanking God for saving you. It'll set the focus for whatever comes your way. In the introduction of the book *Christ in Men…Today*, it reads *"Today. It's the only day we have. Yesterday is a memory. We can't spend tomorrow. This is about living in the moment, not presuming on the future. That's not to say we shouldn't have a plan if God grants us one more day. But too often we live in our plan and not the present."*

God has given each of us unlimited memory capacity. The psalmist says, *"Your Word I have treasured in my heart, that I may not sin against You."* (Ps. 119:11) How much of that capacity can we use for memorizing God's Word? If you don't know Jesus personally, and you want to have a relationship with Him, stop by our "Steps to Salvation" page for a step-by-step outline. You're not imposing on Him. He wants to have a relationship with YOU.

August 25, 2020

What're the odds?

We're in the middle of an election year and everybody has hope that their candidate will win. One side is trying to paint as bleak a picture as they can while blaming the darkness on the incumbent and denying any culpability. The other side is dipping their brush in buckets of hope and painting a bright future with unlimited possibilities.

Just based on initial messaging, (as an ex-advertising man) my advice—to take a phrase from Star Wars—the dark side needs a new ad agency. When did you ever believe that a product promoting doom and gloom would change your life for the better? When was the last time a successful product got that way by bashing its competition? In ad-speak when you don't have a clear, positive message, you're left with two choices. One, you can try to be the cheapest on the shelf. Or, two, you can try to convince your audience how bad your competition is. Neither is a winning strategy.

Think about the Pepsi/Coke challenges. Neither company badmouths the other. They let results (track record) speak for them. Mostly, they don't even mention the competition in their own ads, they focus on, wait for it…their track record. When you don't have a track record, you have to say something and usually, it's negative.

One of the all-time gurus of advertising, Claude Hopkins, in his book *Scientific Advertising* says, "Tell people what to do, not what to avoid."

Think about today's question on odds. How do bookmakers set odds? Isn't it largely based on track record, on what someone or a team has done in the past? Sure, new players can have an impact and up the odds. But looking back is a good gauge of what looking forward will be.

As usual, this blog is about things that matter. What is hope based on? A wish, a dream, a desire for change? What're the odds of your hoped-for thing happening? People buy a lottery ticket, hoping to win. Odds? Millions to one. Weathermen say 50% chance of rain. Duh, they're right either way. As believers in Jesus Christ, our hope is based on God's track record as described in His Word. Never wrong. Never misleading. Always true, the good news AND the bad. Why is that important?

The Bible says, *"Every Word of God is tested..."* (Pro. 30:5) Wouldn't you like that same standard of your politicians? The Bible also says, *"God **cannot** lie"* (Tit. 1:2, emphasis added) That's why we need to pay attention to what God says about the end of days...because they're coming at us like a freight train. What're the odds you'll avoid God's wrath and judgment? Either 100% or zero. It's in your court. If you know Jesus Christ as your Savior, it's 100% you'll avoid God's wrath (1 Thes. 5:9). The darkness and gloom spoken of above will seem like Disneyland ("the happiest place on earth") compared to what awaits those who haven't trusted Christ's death and resurrection to pay for their sin.

If you're not sure and don't like your odds, go to the Appendix "Steps To Salvation" to see a step-by-step roadmap to a relationship with God. Don't wait too long. Just like there's a fixed date for the election, God has fixed an expiration date for each of us (Ps. 139:16). This is the only way I know to stack the odds in our favor. And I like sure things.

August 27, 2020

Birthdays and Divorce

Yesterday was *my* birthday. Today would have been my daughter Staci's 47th. But I buried her just a couple days after her first. Many would say, "how sad." And I did too for a while because I felt the loss, the emptiness. And even now, I can get teary-eyed when I think of her. But I believed then and even more now that **nothing** sneaks up on God and for His glory, He had His reasons. Before she was even born, He planned her days (about 370 of them) according to His will (Ps. 139:16).

If you read my post on August 4, you'll see this was the first of two children God took home. My wife and I certainly had grief and cried many tears over their departures. But over the years, our sadness has turned to joy knowing we'll see them both again when God calls our number.

There is a misconception that up to 80% of marriages end in divorce after the loss of a child. That number is simply not true. In a 2006 study commissioned by The Compassionate Friends, parental divorce following the death of a child was found to be around 16%. The findings were consistent with an earlier study conducted by the group that showed equally low divorce rates among bereaved parents. Interestingly, less than half of those who were divorced following the death of their child (only about 7%) felt that the death had contributed to the disintegration of the marriage. Other factors had more impact on the dissolution.

For my wife and me, the only thing we had to rely on was our faith in God and trusting His Word that He didn't make a mistake or "didn't see that one coming." Whatever the percentage, the grief is real, the coping challenges are real, and even anger at fate, bad luck, or God who "let it happen." But this is a book of good news, not Eeyore-speak.

It's so easy for us to focus primarily on what we can see and know empirically. Spoiler alert: all that will burn up. The invisible world that we can't see with our eyes is what will last forever. That being the case, we probably should spend more time learning about it, understanding it, and embracing the hope that transcends all the shiny objects of this world. How do we do that? Glad you asked.

Of all the perhaps billions of books in the world, there is ONLY ONE that fulfills the truth of learning, understanding, and hope that we need to survive: The Bible, God's eternal Word. If you don't have one, get one. The sooner the better. Make sure it's a "translation", not just a "paraphrase." My favorite is the New American Standard – Revised Edition, but there are other good ones too. If you already have a Bible, are you reading it every day? Memorizing meaningful passages? Applying it to daily living?

The rest of this book is committed to spreading God's Word and encouraging a strong relationship with the One who died to make our future in heaven possible. Also, you can prowl around the "Find a New Path" tab on our website: "*needanewplan.com*", scroll down and read some of the character qualities exampled for us by Jesus Himself. It's all good news available to anyone with a humble heart.

August 29, 2020

Watch where you're going

Never thought I'd trip over my own shoe sole. I guess it's because sometimes I don't pick up my feet far enough and my rubber soles grab and hold the tile or concrete or whatever. I can only remember it happening once when my sole caught the edge of a step and down I went. Fortunately, the ground broke my fall and nothing else broke. Well, maybe my ego a bit.

One time I was backing my 850-lb motorcycle out of my garage down a sloped driveway. While backing I was turning so I didn't back into the street. This one time I turned a little too sharp and I couldn't hold the weight. Down she went onto the crash bars. No damage, but the first thing I did was look around to see if any of my neighbors was watching. I'm sure none of y'all ever do dumb things like that. I used to laugh at "watch your step" signs. Not anymore.

Speaking of watch your step signs, while reading Revelation this morning, I was reminded of all the terrible things coming to a neighborhood near you during a period called "the tribulation," a 7-year period—prophesied millennia ago—when God's wrath is full and ready to be poured out in judgment on an unbelieving world. There are 7 "seal" judgments, 7 "trumpet" judgments, and 7 "bowl" judgments. You can read the entire narrative in Revelation 6-16.

There will be massive death, earthquakes, 1/3 of the earth burned up, 1/3 of the sea turned to blood, 1/3 of the sea creatures die, and 1/3 of ships are destroyed (Rev. 8:8,9). There will be locusts that have stinging power like scorpions that torment man for five months (Rev. (9:2-10). Plagues that kill 1/3 of mankind. All of these are on the horizon. People will be required to get "a mark" on their hand or forehead without which they cannot buy or sell. This mark turns into loathsome and malignant sores on all who get it (Rev. 16:2). And much, much more.

Watch your step…into the future. You can escape all of these judgments **if you're willing to do one thing** that most people aren't. *"Enter through the **narrow gate**; for the gate is **wide** and the way is broad that leads to **destruction**, and there are **many** who enter through it. For the gate is small and the way is **narrow** that leads to **life**, and* *there are few who find it."* (Matt. 7:13,14; emphasis added). It's not hard, and it's free. All these judgments are for everyone who has rejected the way of salvation provided by Jesus Christ through His death and resurrection.

Why would anyone turn down an offer like this? It could be they've never heard the story of how God loved man—the epitome of His creation—so much that He sent His son, Jesus, to restore the relationship that sin had broken. Go to the Appendix "Steps To Salvation" to find out how you can benefit from that love and to see yourself as God sees you.

It could also be that you've heard the story and either don't believe it, think you don't need it because you're good enough (spoiler alert: you aren't), or you're putting it off until you've gotten farther through your bucket list.

You may have bought into the devil's lie that to be saved, in addition to Jesus, you need to amass so many good deeds, or give so much money, or need to be baptized, or any number of other religious sounding lies. Jesus said, *"I am THE way, and THE truth and THE life, no man comes to the Father but through Me"* (John 14:6). There is nothing else necessary but putting your faith into the *finished* work of Christ on the cross.

I have buried a 1-year-old daughter and a 27-year-old son. So I speak from experience when I tell you that tomorrow is NOT GUARANTEED to anybody. If you're not sure whether you're a "saint" or an "ain't" you can be. **God wants you to know the truth**. Jesus said, *"You will know the truth and the truth will set you free"* (John 8:32). Visit the Appendix "Steps To Salvation" for truth on which you can base a life-or-death decision.

Sept 1, 2020

How's *Your* Weather

Technically, Fall isn't here for another 20 days. But it was only 44 degrees when I went to get my paper yesterday. I've lived in the upper Midwest and visited my daughter in Houston, so I don't complain about Colorado Springs weather—cold or hot. Speaking of cold or hot, one thing I love about God's Word is it doesn't pull punches. In Revelation 3:16, "*...because you are lukewarm and neither hot nor cold, I will spit you out of My mouth.*" That's as direct an indictment as you'll get for taking a middle-of-the-road stand for Jesus. And you know He was talking to *church* people.

Anybody have a bucket list? The poet C.T. Studd said it best: "Only one life, 'twill soon be past, only what's done for Christ will last." Life is short. Being ready for tomorrow is crucial. In Colorado, we never went (motorcycle) riding for any distance without taking raingear. We've been caught without it and it's not fun.

We've been given plenty of warning that tribulation—terrible things—are coming to earth. The Bible predicts it in detail...just not the "*hour and day and month and year*" (Rev. 9:15). The main problem with waiting is that it will happen in an instant—the twinkling of an eye (1 Cor. 15:52)—and then it's too late. That's why preparation is critical. Getting ready is not a long, drawn-out process. It happens at the speed of a decision, a decision to trust Jesus Christ to forgive your sins and adopt you into His forever family.

Jesus told the thief on the cross, "*...today you shall be with me in Paradise*" (Luke 23:43). The thief was dying. He had no time to do good deeds or be baptized or anything else, yet Jesus promised "today." Kinda shoots holes in "religious" claims that something has to be added to Jesus to be saved. But that is the devil's strategy, to add requirements of "doing something" to the *finished* work of Christ on the cross. Anyone preaching that message is lying to you. God's gift is free. Like presents on your birthday. You didn't do anything to earn them, and sometimes you probably don't even deserve them. But because your family loves you, you still receive them. God loves *you* and wants *you* in His family. Don't put it off.

If this has piqued your interest, there are two other places in this book to visit: 1) *"Good News Monday"*, 2) Appendix: *Steps to Salvation*. Check them out. If you still have questions, you can contact me at the email in the front of the book.

September 10, 2020

Winners / Losers

Tomorrow is the anniversary of 9/11 (2001). I can't believe it's one year short of two decades since those cowardly attacks on our homeland. Anyone under 20 wasn't even born yet, and it just seems like yesterday to me. Now *that* makes me feel old.

I remember hearing the Twin Towers referred to as "ground zero" many times after the attacks and I got to thinking about the word "zero." It often carries a negative connotation (see: *Beetle Bailey* comic strip), but sometimes it depends on how you ask the question.

I posted *"What are the odds"* on August 25th. For example, If I ask, "What are the odds you'll go to heaven when you die?" The *right* answer will be **100% or zero** depending on your relationship with Jesus Christ. There's no 50/50 or 99/1. It's an all or nothing proposition. If you know Jesus, the odds are **zero** that you'll go to hell, *"Therefore there is now no condemnation for those who are in Christ Jesus."* (Rom. 8:1; see blog entry "Good News Monday")

God's plan is not a "zero-sum" game (somebody wins, somebody loses). Actually it's not a game at all, it's life and death serious. Life is filled with zero-sum situations. A company has only so many positions to fill. Somebody wins somebody loses. Sports championships have only one winner…and one (or many) losers. But God is not like that. It's like a barker at the circus, "Everybody plays. Everybody wins." With God's approach, everybody *can* play and everybody *can* win. The Bible says, *"For God so loved the world that He gave His only begotten Son, that **whoever** believes in Him **shall not perish**, but have eternal life."* (John 3:16, emphasis added)

Jesus was probably the best storyteller of all time and His stories *always* had eternal significance. He told a story (parable) about a man who was preparing for a journey and called three of his servants and entrusted his possessions to them.

To one he gave five talents, to another two and another one **according to their abilities**. The 5-talent guy and the 2-talent guy went and doubled their master's value. The 1-talent guy blew it. Both the five and two guys were rewarded the same *"Well done, good and* *faithful slave. You were faithful with a few things, I will put you in charge of many things."* (Matt. 25:14-29)

Notice the 5-talent guy now had 10 talents, 250% more than the 2-talent guy (now 4 talents), but their reward and praise from their master was identical. Why? Because they performed faithfully according to their *(individual)* abilities. God didn't hold 2-talent guy accountable to accomplish 5-talent guy's assignment when he didn't have the same abilities.. We are all gifted uniquely. We're not part of a zero-sum game. I don't have to lose so you can win. We both win if we're trustworthy with God's riches.

So what's the point of all this? Allow a couple examples first. When Peter asked Jesus *"Lord, and what about this man* [John]?" Jesus' reply was to get Peter to focus on himself not anyone else, *"If I want him to remain until I come, **what is that to you? You follow Me.**"* (John 21:21,22) And the prophet Micah makes it clear to the Israelites, *"He has told you, **O man**, what is good; and what does the Lord require of **you** but to do justice, to love kindness, and to walk humbly with your God?"* (Micah 6:8; emphasis added)

In God's economy we can **all** be **winners** as long as we do it His way. There **will be losers** because not everyone wants to or will do it His way. Too bad. Don't discard this as mere ramblings, **it's THE TRUTH**.

Our focus needs to be on ourselves and what God has called us to do. If we're committed to that calling and faithful in its execution, we can expect to hear, "well done" when we meet Jesus face to face. If we're not **eagerly looking** for His return, some self-examination is in order. Paul told the Corinthian church, *"Test yourselves to see if you are in the faith; examine yourselves!"* (II Cor. 13:5) and to the Philippians he wrote, *"For our citizenship is in heaven from which also we **eagerly wait for a Savior, the Lord Jesus Christ**."* (Phil. 3:20)

Make sure you're ready. The time is short. Hope to see you there.

September 12, 2020

Dollars and Sense

The movie *Jerry Maguire* (1996) turned the line "show me the money" into an entry in our modern lexicon. We've all heard TV cop shows say, "follow the money" and we'll find the mind behind the crime. That's probably good advice in today's topsy-turvy world of political positions that seem contrary to common sense and rational thought.

The Apostle Paul wrote about today's irrational, senseless condition 2,000 years ago in his letter to the Romans. "(18) *For the wrath of God is revealed from heaven against all ungodliness and unrighteousness of **men who suppress the truth** in unrighteousness...(28) And just as they **did not** see fit to **acknowledge God** any longer, **God gave them over to a depraved mind**, to do those things which are not proper.*" (Romans 1:18,28) The verses filling the gap between these two give an incredibly accurate picture of where our society is today. Sin, apart from repentance and forgiveness through Jesus Christ, always gets worse, just like the second law of thermodynamics. Chaos never reverts to order. Read the "gap" verses in Romans 1 from 18 through 32 and you'll see for yourself a downward spiral of attitudes and activities exactly mirroring our current societal trends.

I've been asked questions regarding our current condition, the likelihood of a "return to normal" and how soon, "Are we in the "last days?" and other similar questions. **No one** has any special knowledge from God other than what's written in His Word. Many have observed our society slipping steadily into a morass of unrighteousness—sin—for decades, from which there will be no return...until Jesus rules on earth in the Millennial Kingdom (Rev. 20:1-6).

For those who think one political party or the other can change the hatred, violence and total disregard of law and order, they're dreaming. The ONLY THING that could restore the U.S. to the country our founders envisioned is repentance in a scope I haven't seen in my lifetime.

I'm not saying it *couldn't* happen, but...here are the requirements, "**If**...*My people...**humble themselves** and **pray** and **seek My face** and **turn from their wicked ways**, then I will...forgive their sin and will* *heal their land.*" (2 Chron. 2:13,14; emphasis added) Like I said, it *could* happen. But apart from Divine intervention, it won't. How do I know? "*Then the Lord saw that the wickedness of man was great on the earth, and that **every intent of the thoughts of his heart was only evil continually.**" (Gen.6:5; emphasis added)* And that was man's legacy way back in Genesis (***before*** and ***the cause of*** the flood). Man's heart hasn't changed over the approximately 6,000 years we've been on earth. Jeremiah confirms that (give or take) fifteen centuries later, "*The heart is **more deceitful** than all else and is **desperately sick**; who can understand it?*" (Jer. 17:9; emphasis added)

My hope is that there will be some who read this who wonder what is happening and worry because they have no hope anchored in the One Rock that can do anything about it. If that's you and you don't know Jesus Christ as your *personal* Lord and Savior, get a copy of the book, *Christ in Men...Today.* You'll find 52 weeks of character-building messages to build your spiritual muscles. If you are ready to have Jesus transform your life, visit the Appendix: *Steps To Salvation.* You can also contact us for prayer or questions by email. Let us know if God has spoken to your heart. It's a great encouragement to us.

September 17, 2020

God's 12-Step Program

Everybody has a top-10 list of something: cars, songs, places to live, easy meals. God has a top-10 list. They're called commandments. You know, thou shall, and thou shall not? Alcoholics Anonymous has a 12-step program to change lives for those battling the demon rum. Guess what? God has a 12-step program too. The steps are rungs on a ladder of promise. Any ladder with twelve rungs must be able to reach a lofty height. This one is no exception. If you can do it, God has promised that you'll *"never be shaken."* (Psalm 15:5)

Is that a good goal? Ask yourself, "What shakes people in general and me specifically?" I believe fear tops the list, and the list of fears is long. The following are from a list of top 100 fears. For most of us, many of these seem silly, but for those who suffer from one or more, they're very real. Here is just a sample. Fear of failure (atychiphobia, #15) and its opposite, fear of success (achiemephobia, # 30), fear of public speaking (glossophobia, # 13), fear of spiders (arachnophobia, #1), and it goes on and on.

When commercial buildings are built, the foundations are dug down until either bedrock is hit or it's deep enough for footings that won't be shaken. What are you building your life on? If it's not The Rock—Jesus Christ—then the wood, hay, and stubble you're using has no ability to protect you from the things that go bump in the night.

Before I list the twelve, it's important to know that these are not a magic elixir, not a rabbit's foot or wishbone, and not a "one and done," something to do once and voila, you're successful. They are the very Word of God, intended as a **way of life** in obedience to and faith in the One who sets the rules. Also know this, that success in this area is not measured by a life free of trials, free of temptation, or free of tragedy. But, and this is an important but, it does guarantee that you have Someone watching your "six" that has the power, ability, and desire to protect you.

God's promise (never be shaken) is for the one who: (Ps. 15:1-5)

1   Exhibits integrity (v.2)
2   Does justice (v.2)
3   Speaks truth (v.2)

4	Does not slander (v.3)
5	Does not harm his fellow man (v.3)
6	Does not reproach (rebuke or disapprove) his friend (v.3)
7	Views a reprobate as despised (v.4)
8	Honors the people of God (v.4)
9	Holds himself accountable (v.4)
10	Commits and does not change (v.4)
11	Deals fairly without greed (v.5)
12	Cannot be bought or bribed (v.5)

Nobody said it was going to be easy, but remember that you have a Helper who is with you forever (John14:16), you're not in this war alone. Remember James Bond always ordered his drink *shaken* not *stirred*. But as believers in the Lord Jesus Christ, we won't be shaken when we are stirred by the Holy Spirit to love and obedience to our Father who **always** keeps His promises.

September 18, 2020

Out of the Heart

You ever have one of those days when you open your mouth and you can't believe what you just said? If only you had a 7-second delay like radio broadcasters and could squash it before anybody heard and you had to figure out how to get your foot out of your mouth. Today's thought was spawned by Democrat Vice-Presidential Candidate Sen. Kamala Harris. In a campaign stop in Arizona, before she could censor her thought, here's what came out: "In a Harris administration with Joe Biden as president…" Oops.

Why does that happen when we think we're so clever at hiding our deception, our motives, our true thoughts? God has designed into man a truth-serum-like filter that, in unguarded moments, allows the truth to escape. Listen to a couple descriptions from the Book of Truth. *"The heart of the righteous ponders how to answer, but the mouth of the wicked pours out evil things."* (Prov. 15:28) *"For the mouth speaks out of that which fills the heart."* (Matt. 12:34) *"The good man out of the good treasure of his heart brings forth what is good, and the evil man out of the evil treasure brings forth what is evil, for his mouth speaks from that which fills his heart."* (Luke 6:45) And even if you think you've gotten away with hiding the truth, one more. *"Would not God find this out? For He knows the secrets of the heart."* (Ps. 44:21)

Remember when your mom told you, "If you don't have something nice to say, don't say anything?" That's only the outward solution. It doesn't do anything to clean up the source. Notice the verses are statements of fact. They are not what ifs or conditioned on circumstances. If you want good stuff to come out, you gotta have good stuff inside to start with. It is what it is.

James gives a command to deal with this issue, *"Draw near to God and He will draw near to you. Cleanse your hands, you sinners; and purify your hearts, you double-minded."* (Jas. 4:8) Cleansing hands was a ritual performed by Old Testament priests before approaching God. The term "sinners" is only used of unbelievers. Purify deals with the inner thoughts, motives, and desires of the heart. So we know we're supposed to do this. The question is how?

Paul has the answer in his letter to the Philippians, *"Finally, breth-ren, whatever is true, whatever is honorable, whatever is right, what-ever is pure, whatever is lovely, whatever is of good repute, if there is any excellence and if anything worthy of praise, dwell on these things."* (Phil. 4:8) Thinking of this reminds me of a Louis Armstrong song, *"What a Wonderful World."* Wouldn't it be great to believe eve-rything spoken by politicians, attorneys, preachers? In the 1997 movie starring Jim Carrey, *"Liar Liar,"* Carrey couldn't lie for 24 hours be-cause of his son's birthday wish. We all laughed but it was sad recog-nizing just how many times and how easy it was for him to lie.

So what's our takeaway today? Are politicians going to stop ly-ing? Will the Pope convert to Protestantism? No. Our ONLY hope is for sinners to turn to Jesus Christ and be changed from the inside, be given a *new* heart. *"Moreover, I will give you a new heart and put a new spirit within you; and I will remove the heart of stone from your flesh and give you a heart of flesh."* (Ezek. 36:26) If *you* need a new heart, turn to the Appendix *Steps to Salvation* and go through the list of 9 steps to understand your predicament and God's solution. If you need more information, you can contact us through the email in the front of this book.

September 21, 2020

Better Than Gold?

Gold has always been a highly prized possession. Just in the first two books of the Bible, it's mentioned nearly 100 times. The temple was adorned with gold. The ark of the covenant was covered with gold. The temple utensils were gold. Abraham was rich in gold. When the Israelites were getting ready to leave Egypt, the men and women asked their neighbors for articles of silver and gold and *"thus you will plunder the Egyptians."* (Ex. 3:22; 11:2)

In more modern times, the California Gold Rush brought many to the front hoping to strike it rich. Many did. But many also failed. Greed spawned thefts and murders in order to own the yellow metal. If you can believe the movie depictions of the era, booze flowed freely, and gambling and prostitution were widespread. In the last ten years we've seen the price of gold range from just over a thousand dollars an ounce to over two thousand. From 1934 to 1969 the price of gold was fairly steady at around $34 an ounce. Today it's over $1,900 an ounce.

Most of the gold mined today—about 75%--ends up in jewelry. The rest is spread over minted coins, electronic components (excellent conductor of electricity), medicine and dentistry, computers and cell phones and space technology. Because of its rarity and, apart from some wild swings in assumed value due to speculators, it has always been accepted as a stable currency.

But God doesn't want His people to focus on gold for two reasons. First, *"Your gold and your silver have rusted; and their rust will be a witness against you and will consume your flesh like fire."* (James 5:3) And second, He has something better…and it's free. *"The law of the Lord is perfect…the testimony of the Lord is sure…the precepts of the Lord are right…the commandment of the Lord is pure…the fear of the Lord is clean…the judgments of the Lord are true…**they are more desirable than gold, yes, than much fine gold**…moreover, by them Your servant is warned; in keeping them there is **great reward**."* (Ps. 19:7-11; emphasis added)

I firmly believe that many of God's people today do not place high value on God's Word. It's like they've gotten their ticket for the Glory

Train punched and that's all they care about. If that weren't true, today's church would be more relevant, more powerful as a societal influencer and more prominent in the daily lives of believers. God's Word would occupy a large part of our hearts, not just a space on a dusty shelf. It would prevent deceptive theology from sneaking into our churches. We would be more like the Bereans: "*Now these [Bereans] were more noble-minded than those in Thessalonica, for they received the word with **great eagerness**, examining the Scriptures **daily** to see whether these things were so*." (Acts 17:11)

Are we eager to study God's Word or is it a drag? Do we rationalize with thoughts like "It's so hard to understand" or "That's the Pastor's job?" Jesus said to His disciples, "*If anyone **loves Me**, he will **keep My word**... (24) He who **does not love Me** does **not keep My words**"* (John 14:23,24). Simple question: How can we keep Jesus' words if we don't know them? How do we know them if we don't read and study the Bible? The Psalmist said, "*Your Word is very pure, therefore Your servant **loves it**.*" (Ps. 119:140)

What else can you think of that is "more desirable than **much fine gold**?" Jesus told a parable about a guy who found a treasure hidden in a field (Matt.13:44). He was overjoyed, went, and sold all he had and bought the field. The treasure is a picture of salvation. Salvation, we're told, comes by grace through faith (Eph. 2:8), "...*faith comes from hearing, and hearing by the word of Christ.*" (Rom. 10:17) So if you're not in love with The Word of God, you should examine yourself to see if you have been given the gift of salvation. A good tree bears good fruit.

If you don't know for sure that you're a new creature in Christ (2 Cor. 5:17), turn to the Appendix *Steps to Salvation* for an overview of your condition and future from God's perspective. Thanks for reading.

September 22, 2020

Talk to Yourself

Used to be if you talked to yourself you were headed for the padded cell. But D. Martyn Lloyd-Jones (1899-1981) spawned the idea of talking to yourself instead of listening to yourself in this quote, "Have you realized that most of your unhappiness in life is due to the fact that you are listening to yourself instead of talking to yourself?" What does that really mean?

We who know The Truth are not much different from the world in this respect; we listen to our own grumbling and complaining, and it colors our outlook. And, like Lloyd-Jones' quote, that's where most of our unhappiness comes from.

See Yourself as God Sees You

Rather than that, we should take our example from King David. Listen to his internal "conversations" with himself. *"Why are you in despair O my soul? And why have you become disturbed within me?* ***Hope*** *in God, for I shall again praise Him for the help of His presence."* (Ps. 42:5 and repeated in Ps. 43:5) And another conversation, *"My soul, wait in silence for God only, for my* ***hope*** *is from Him."* (Ps. 62:5) Do you see the common thread? Whatever was going on in his life, David never lost **hope** that his God was near enough and strong enough to deliver him...if that was His will.

I'm not saying that we should stick our heads in the sand and deny current events and circumstances. But I *am* saying that awareness of evil shouldn't cause fear. We *are* on the winning team. What are we telling ourselves? What kind of counsel do we give ourselves? Solomon said, *"The way of a fool is right in his own eyes, but a wise man is he who listens to counsel"* (Prov. 12:15). Are we giving ourselves wise counsel?

What are some specifics we can tell ourselves? God loves us. He has forgiven us. He has not and will not abandon us. He has prepared a place for us in heaven and it's secure. What are all these based on? Isn't it the hope He has placed in our hearts? Listen to a couple promises we can take to the bank.

"Behold, ***the eye of the Lord is on those who fear Him***, *on those who hope for His lovingkindness."* (Ps. 33:18)

"Do not let your heart envy sinners but live in the fear of the Lord always. (v18) Surely there is a future, and **your hope will not be cut off***.*" (Prov. 23:17,18)

"Let us **hold fast the confession of our hope** *without wavering, for* **He who promised is faithful***.*" (Heb. 10:23)

Memorizing Scripture is an excellent way to fill the storehouse of things to tell ourselves. God is faithful. If He said it, He did it or He will do it. We need to be like Paul who kept his eyes on the prize (Phil. 3:14) and didn't let his circumstances drag him down.

We may be tempted to think that our circumstances or environment have caused our predicament and we're helpless in its wake. Not true. Adam and Eve lived in a perfect environment…and still sinned. No, it's a heart problem and until God replaces our heart of stone with one of flesh (Ezek. 36:26) none of this makes sense. If you take nothing else from this, remember that our future is built on hope in the one thing that will always be rock-solid, faithful, and true: God Himself and His Word.

Talk to yourself often, even before your feet hit the floor each morning. And fill your life with messages of hope in the **One who cannot lie** (Tit. 1:2). If you're a little unsure of whether you qualify for these promises, check out the Appendix *Steps to Salvation* and know for sure. Thanks again for reading.

September 26, 2020

Two Sides of a Coin

Heads or tails? Win or lose in a 50/50 proposition. If the stakes are small, it's no big deal to lose the toss. In football overtime it can sometimes mean the game if you get the ball first. What are you flipping the coin of life to answer? You've heard it said that not to decide is a decision, the results of which you can't predict and probably won't like. When life comes at you like a freight train, it's good to have a plan and a backup. Instant gratification that hasn't planned for the future often leaves us with neither.

Like the coin, God has two sides. Listen to the Psalmist(s): Side 1 *"For the Lord is good; His lovingkindness is everlasting and His faithfulness to all generations."* (Ps. 100:5) And side 2 *"Therefore I swore in My anger truly they shall not enter into My rest."* (Ps. 95:11) Does that sound like the same God? There are many similar verses to reinforce both sides of this "coin."

Unlike the coin used for decision making, the yes/no decision to know and obey your Creator is not random. Paul's letter to the church in Rome is very clear describing their "side two"—the charges against them—and the justified *why* of God's anger. Let's look. *"For the wrath of God is revealed from heaven against all ungodliness and unrighteousness of men **who suppress the truth** in unrighteousness, **because** that which is known about God is **evident within them;** for **God made it evident to them.** For **since the creation of the world** His invisible **attributes,** His eternal **power** and divine **nature, have been clearly seen,** being **understood through what has been made,** so that **they are without excuse.** For even though **they knew God,** they **did not honor Him** as God or give thanks, but **they became futile in their speculations,** and their foolish heart was darkened. **Professing to be wise, they became fools**..."* (Rom. 1:18-22)

Paul doesn't pull any punches. He tells it like it is because the most loving thing you can do is tell the truth to those who are perishing. I'm not advocating beating people over the head with God's Word. The Bible tells us to let our speech "always be with grace" (Col. 4:6) so *we* don't offend our hearers. But we are not to water down the message that *"the gate is wide and the **way is broad** that leads to destruction,* and there are **many** who enter through it. For the gate is small and the **way is narrow** that leads to life, and there are **few** who find it." (Matt. 7:13,14)

If you're not sure which path you're on, don't be discouraged by the words *many* and *few*. This is where the randomness of flipping a coin is eliminated. In Joshua's farewell address to the Israelites, he gives them the same choice we have, "*If it is disagreeable in your sight to serve the Lord, **choose for yourselves** today whom you will serve: whether the gods which your fathers served which were beyond the river, or the gods of the Amorites in whose land you are living; but as for me and my house, we will serve the Lord.*" (Josh. 24:15) In today's language it might sound something like this, "If you don't want to serve your Creator, decide today whom (or what) you will serve: whether the (little g) god of popularity, or the god of money and power, or more likely, the god of self. As for me, I'm all in for the one true God and His Son, Jesus Christ."

Remember, there are consequences for the choices we make. Hindsight provides me with a crystal-clear picture, video actually, of some of the bad choices I've made. I thank God that He has a "side 1" that includes me. If you'd like that assurance, visit the Appendix *Steps to Salvation* found in the back of this book. Thanks for reading.

September 29, 2020

Why Wait?

You ever let a friendship lapse for months, even years, and all of a sudden you need a favor from that person? You feel a little sheepish, don't you? What will they think? Why is he calling now? What does he need? And you wonder if there's anything left of the relationship.

I suggest, that for many of us, our relationship with God is a lot like that. We treat Him like a genie or Santa Claus, we only seek Him out when we need something. The Israelites were like that. Here's one sample: *"They [the Israelites] were hungry and thirsty; their soul fainted within them. **Then** they cried out to the Lord in their trouble; He delivered them out of their distresses."* (Ps. 107:5,6; emphasis added) **Four times** in this Psalm (v.6,13,19,28) it says, "**Then** they cried out to the Lord." The sad thing is that each time it was only AFTER their stubbornness and rejection of God's ways had gotten them into dire circumstances: v.5 "They were hungry and thirsty," v.12 "They stumbled and there was none to help," v.18 "they drew near to the gates of death," v.26 "their soul melted away in their misery."

Had God forgotten them? No. EVERY time they cried out, it says, "He delivered them out of their distresses (v.6), He saved them out of their distresses (v.13,19), He brought them out of their distresses (v.28)." Why did they wait until things got bad to seek their provider, protector, deliverer, their friend? I have a note in the margin of my Bible to remind myself "repent early." I'm thankful for the perspective of history. It's much better to learn from other people's mistakes.

I've thought to myself, "God, I've got this one. You take care of the important stuff." But is that the relationship *He* wants? Not when He tells us, "…casting **all** your anxieties on Him because He cares for you" (1 Pet.5:7). There's a caveat in the preceding verse that often stands in our way, *"Therefore **humble yourselves** under the mighty hand of God, that He may exalt you at the proper time."* Can I see a show of hands? How many of us like the idea of humbling ourselves? I didn't raise mine either. Ask yourself, "Doesn't learning *anything* require humility?" It means admitting that I don't know everything. What could be better than learning to obey God?

We spend tons of money to "improve" ourselves. We go to gyms, buy the latest fashion, eat trendy food. And in themselves, there's nothing wrong with those things. But hear what Paul tells the younger Timothy, "*For bodily discipline is only of little profit, but godliness is profitable for all things, since it holds promise for the present life and also for the life to come.*" (1 Tim. 4:8)

I believe the Israelites' hesitancy to call on God was due to the guilt they felt over their disobedience. Here's a thought, a challenge. Rather than wait to call on God, why not keep the relationship fresh? Why not keep our sin account short, as in, don't put off dealing with it? Repent. The longer we wait, the more likely God's attention-getting measures will be harsh, harsher, then harshest.

You say, that sounds good but how do I do it? Start with reading the Bible. The Psalmist says, "*Establish Your Word to Your servant as that which produces reverence for You.*" (Ps. 119:38) You don't get to know anyone without spending time with them. God is no different. You don't learn to revere Him without knowing Him. Thankfully, He gave us the Christian user's guide. Spending time in His Word is the best way to know Him. It's the ONLY source of truth cover to cover that will last throughout eternity. Jesus said, "*Heaven and earth will pass away, but My Words **will not pass away**.*" (Mark 13:31)

In addition to reading, we need to spend time talking not "to" God, but "with" God. We won't hear Him audibly. But He speaks clearly and sometimes loudly to our spirit. After all, He lives in us **if we've surrendered our lives to Jesus Christ**. If you haven't, check out the "Steps to Salvation" Appendix in the back of this book.

One final thought: DON'T WAIT, it's later than you think. You can't spend tomorrow. As always, thanks for reading.

October 2, 2020

It's Not About Me

What do emcees, judges, debate moderators, and preachers all have in common? They're in the public eye. They direct whatever goes on in their venue. They have a lot of authority to make sure things go well. But THEY ARE NOT THE STAR OF THE SHOW. You might call each one a "pointer." What do pointers do? Pointers point. Emcees point to guests, performers, award recipients and others. Judges point to the law and enforce it. Debate moderators point to the debaters and see that they are treated equally with respect to time and difficulty of questions. The preacher's job is to point his listeners to Jesus Christ. They may all have charisma and audiences like them. But when you're in the public eye, the bigger the audience the bigger the temptation to think "it's about me, I'm the star here." Watch out pride is lurking to make you fall. (Prov. 16:18)

We're told to "love God and love your neighbor." (Matt. 22:37,39) Sometimes when looking to define something, it's helpful to see what it *is not*. Paul has a list of "love is nots," "**not jealous, does not brag, not arrogant**, doesn't act unbecomingly, **does not seek its own**, not provoked…" (1 Cor. 13:4,5) Paul goes on in the next two verses with the "dos." "…**rejoices** with the truth; **bears** all things, **believes** all things, **hopes** all things, **endures** all things.

In the secular world, we see example after example of how not to act…in public or any time. You can hardly blame someone in a position of leadership for missing the mark of the "is nots" when they are constantly bombarded by "the other side." But consider Moses after leaving Egypt. We're told that "the people" (probably over two million of them) quarreled with him over leading them to a place without water. But remember, Moses was following God in the cloud and pillar of fire. So the Israelites were really grumbling against God. There's an interesting parenthetical comment in Numbers 12:3, *"Now the man Moses was very humble, more than any man who was on the face of the earth."*

Most of us are drawn to humility as well as kindness, and justice displayed in others. But because we're prone to put ourselves first, we struggle to attain these qualities in ourselves. Did you know we're commanded to *"do justice, love kindness, and walk humbly with God?"* Micah tells us *"the Lord requires it of you."* (Micah 6:8)

Could it be we seek the limelight because we're insecure with our lot in life and we're jealous of those who seem to have it all? Or maybe we're angry because we've busted our hump and not gotten the recognition we think we deserve. Whatever the cause of our dissatisfaction, we need to own it then discard it because it shows that our trust is in ourselves and not in God who doesn't allow anything to come our way that doesn't fit His plan for us. Paul tells us that he *"learned to **be content** in whatever circumstances I am…humble means or prosperity…being filled or going hungry…having abundance or suffering need."* (Phil. 4:11,12) And in the very next verse he says, *"I can do all things through Him [Christ] who strengthens me."*

As believers in Jesus Christ, our job is simply to glorify Him. We're told, *"Whether, then, you eat or drink or **whatever you do, do all to the glory of God**.* (1 Cor. 10:31) Sometimes God gets glory when He abundantly blesses us with material things because He knows we can handle it correctly and not take credit for it. Other times, He gets glory when we stand firm against the pummeling schemes of the devil while the world watches our faithfulness. Whatever means whatever.

If we can learn and practice keeping the Lord Jesus as the star of the show instead of ourselves, our lives will be filled with peace, the world will see Christianity as it should look, and we can expect to hear "well done good and faithful servant" when we see Jesus face to face. If you're not in the "whatever you do" camp or think you are but aren't sure, visit the "Steps to Salvation" Appendix to get God's heart on the matter. Thanks for reading.

October 4, 2020

Can You Handle the Truth?

You probably remember the line from the 1992 movie *A Few Good Men,* in which Jack Nicholson's character, Colonel Jessup, screams at Tom Cruise's character, Lt. Kaffee, "You can't handle the truth." It has worked its way into American culture without much thought given to how prescient the message. I was reminded of this while reading the 9th chapter of John.

Jesus has just healed a blind beggar and the Pharisees have him in for questioning…a second time because they didn't believe him the first time even after his parents confirmed he had been born blind. But being afraid of the religious leaders and the threat of being thrown out of the synagogue, the parents weaseled out of giving credit to Jesus. So the son is subjected to insinuations of his veracity. And like Colonel Jessup, he's becoming frustrated, so he says, *"I told you already and you did not listen; why do you want to hear it again? You do not want to become His disciples too, do you?"* (John 9:27)

Here's the thing about truth, especially when it conflicts with our preconceived beliefs, it is a direct hit on our pride and like Colonel Jessup's assumption that Lt. Kaffee couldn't handle the truth, the Pharisees couldn't either. They chose to defend their pride with this comment, *"You were born entirely in sins, and **are you teaching us?**"* (v.34)

Being on the receiving end of a truth-empowered word, whether from our spouse, our boss, our child, or someone we don't like or respect. Our pride is hurt, we're embarrassed, we feel shame and maybe even anger at the messenger. We've all heard the phrase, "don't shoot the messenger." But pride and anger don't mix well and that's exactly how we feel. If we're the messenger, and don't want to be shot, we are to "speak the truth in love." (Eph. 4:15) Do we always do that? Or could our delivery use a little softening? Not the message. The delivery.

Have you ever wondered why so many in public office today are offended by the truth? The Bible lays it out pretty clearly in second Thessalonians 2:10-12: *"…and with all the deception of wickedness **for those who perish**, because they did not receive the **love of the truth*** *so as to be saved. For this reason **God will send** upon them **a deluding influence** so that **they will believe what is false** …in order that they all may be judged **who did not believe the truth**, but **took pleasure in wickedness**.*"

Rejecting God's truth has **eternal consequences**. Jesus said, "you will know the truth and the truth will make you free." (John 8:32) What truth should we embrace? Here's a 30,000-foot view. If nobody has told you this before, either they don't love you enough or they need this message too. Remember, don't shoot the messenger. **There is a God**. God hates sin. **You sin**. Sin separates you from God. Sin causes (eternal) death. **God loves you** (anyway) and **sent His son Jesus to die for your sin**. God's gift of **salvation is *free*.** Pride keeps you from accepting this gift. Anything else? Lots. But you don't get the rest until after you walk through the door to salvation, when you've come to Jesus in humility, told God you agree with Him that you are a sinner and can't save yourself, and ask for His mercy.

When you do that, your future in heaven with Jesus and all who have taken these words to heart will be beyond imagination. But here's the thing; old habits die hard and you've got an enemy—the devil—who hates God and His children and will do everything he can to dissuade you and lie to you to keep you out of heaven. If this has piqued your interest, go to the Appendix "*Steps to Salvation*" for a more detailed presentation of the truth you seek. Thanks for reading.

October 5, 2020

Are You in the Game?

What's the difference between a church pew and a football sideline? Generally speaking, everybody on the bench in football is trained and anxious to get in the game. Not so much church pews today. Many people, young and old, sitting in church think their attendance is all that is required to get their ticket punched. They just have to show up, smile, and shake a few hands and their weekly commitment has been fulfilled. But how is that obeying Christ's final command to "go and make disciples?" (Matt. 28:19)

I don't have exact numbers, but whenever I've asked for a show of hands in a group as to who has shared the gospel with another person and led them to salvation—the first step in discipleship—the response is, well let's just say, disappointing. Many are timid because they don't feel adequately trained. I understand that. But my question is, "How long have you known Jesus?" Remember the Samaritan woman at the well? She *immediately* went and told the men about Jesus. They went to see for themselves and many believed. (John 4:29,39-42)

We don't have to know all the answers to share what has happened to us. The blind beggar in yesterday's post said to the Pharisees, "...all I know is once I was blind but now I see." (John 9:25) Isn't that our condition? We were blind to the truth of the gospel and now we see/know Jesus.

Where does the timidity—call it what it is, fear—to share the good news come from? Isn't it because we're more concerned with what *people* think of us than what *God* thinks of us? Jesus tells us in the Gospel of Mark, *"For **whoever is ashamed of Me** and My words in this adulterous and sinful generation, **the Son of Man will also be ashamed of him** when He comes in the glory of His Father with the holy angels."* (Mark 8:38) Or could it be that we're not sure what we believe. Did God really create the universe in six literal days? Was there really a worldwide flood? Did a donkey really talk? Was there really a virgin birth? Is Jesus really God? The answer to all those questions (and many more) is YES, REALLY.

Fact #1: The Bible is truth, cover to cover. Everything in it is true. That's the starting point for the confidence to share. If we have doubts about that, maybe we've been deluding ourselves about our own salvation. Being in a church doesn't make you a Christian any more that being in a garage makes you a Corvette. The Bible says, *"you will know them by their fruits."* (Matt.7:15-20)

Fact #2: If you've really had a life-changing experience with Jesus Christ, then you have a story to tell that nobody can refute. It's your story, your life. You know what you were before you met Jesus. You know what you are now. That's your truth. Don't be afraid to tell it. Memorize a few key verses to support what you're saying. For starters, John 3:16 *"God loved the world so much He gave His Son to die in our place."* Rom 3:23 *"All have sinned..."* We're separated from God by our sin. Rom. 6:23 *"The wages of sin is death."* We can't cover those wages. Left on our own, we'll all die (eternally). 2 Cor. 5:17 *"If anyone is in Christ, he is a new creature. The old is dead, the new [life in Christ] replaced it."* And there are many more to choose from. Make them part of your own story. A message prepared in the mind only reaches another mind, but a message prepared in the heart, reaches another heart.

Fact #3: Here are a couple very good resources to learn a way to share your new life story: evangelismexplosion.org and wayofthemaster.com. Spend some time browsing them to find what works for you. Go with confidence because God empowers His word. Listen, *"My word...will not return to Me empty, without accomplishing what I desire and without succeeding in the matter for which I sent it."* (Isa. 55:11) Helpful hint: The power is in the word itself, not your presentation of it. Let it out to do its job.

Fact #4: Pray for those in your family and your group of friends before and after you share the gospel message with them. The Bible says, *"...the prayer of a righteous man can accomplish much."* (James 5:16) If you know Jesus as your Lord and Savior, then you qualify for this promise. No, you're not righteous on your own and yes, you still sin. But when God looks at you, He sees the righteousness of Christ abiding in you. (Phil. 3:9)

Thanks for reading. Come back often to be fed another helping of God's truth.

October 7, 2020

What's in a name?

Anybody get a name like Chunk, Schnoz, or Dumbo hung on them in grammar school that you didn't like but it stuck for a while, maybe even a long while? Today, I'd like to suggest we look at our uniqueness from God's perspective. After all, He made us exactly as He wanted, nose, ears, all of it.

Isaiah 43:1 tells us, "*...I have redeemed you; I have **called you by name**; you are Mine!*" Think of the implications of that statement. God knows our name. He also knows everything about us, and not only us but every person who ever lived. We can't hide from Him although Jonah tried, and God sent a "great fish" to swallow him up until he came to his senses. (Jon. 1:17) If we know Jesus as our Lord and Savior, this should be a comfort to us. We're not going to get lost in the crowd. The Psalmist tells us in Psalm 33:18, "*...the eye of the Lord is on those who fear Him.*" That's only a scary thought if you're trying to hide from God.

God knows us. He made us unique, and has a purpose for each of us that will be different from others. Peter, one of Jesus' inner circle, had to be reminded of that when he was concerned about what Jesus had planned for fellow inner-circle disciple John. Peter asks Jesus, "Lord, what about this man [John]?" Jesus tells Peter that it's not his concern, "*...if I want him to remain until I come, **what is that to you? You follow Me!**"* (Jn. 21:22) In a polite way He was saying "that's John's business, you take care of Peter."

That's a good reminder for us today when we have our hands full with our own plate. Certainly our mission *involves* other people but we're not responsible for the outcome of our obedience. Some of us plant, some water, but it's God who reaps the harvest. We're only measured on our faithfulness to Christ's calling, not how many turn from a life of evil to one of righteousness.

Sometimes we try to hide from God in our busyness. Many of us categorize or pigeon-hole our lives into tightly sealed compartments consisting of "religious" activities and "secular" activities. Our Sundays, at least the mornings, are reserved for church. The rest of the week we're busy with work, kid duties, all sorts of activities. How does that jibe with God's command? *"Whether, then, you eat or drink or whatever you do, do all to the glory of God."* (1 Cor. 10:31) If "all" means all, then is there really even a "secular" category? Hmmm.

If this sounds interesting to you but you have questions, take a few minutes and visit our "Steps to Salvation" page in the appendix in the back of the book. Thanks for visiting. Browse our site: need-anewplan.com. It's full of good news. Hope to see you again soon.

October 10, 2020

Guided by Circumstances

There's a fine line between foolishness and trust. They are differentiated by the *object* of our trust. If we're trusting fate or karma or universal randomness, we are fools because in essence we've said, "there is no God." (Psalm 53:1) On the other hand, if we're trusting in the One God, creator of heaven and earth, the One who knows the end from the beginning (Isa. 46:10), then we make our plans, we're disciplined to work them, but we have no control over the outcome. Our faith in this God allows us to go with the flow and not become disillusioned when *our* plan doesn't work the way we want it to, knowing there's something better waiting. Because of this, we can still be filled with God's peace.

How can this be? Our natural reaction would be frustration, maybe anger, and likely discouragement over wasted time and money. But that's the problem. That would be our *natural* reaction. The Bible says, *"But a natural man does not accept the things of the Spirit of God, for they are foolishness to him."* (1 Cor. 2:14)

If we know Jesus as our Savior, then we have the Spirit of God living in us and we can accept God's solutions and God's circumstances confident that God is watching our "six" and He doesn't allow anything that isn't in our best interest and for His glory. It may not seem like it when we're in the trial, but that's the difference between trusting God and just hoping for the best. If we knew how something would turn out before it began, it would be cheating. But knowing the One Who not only knows but controls how everything turns out isn't. It's called faith.

I love the Book of Genesis. It's a must read for anyone who wants to see into the heart of God. Abraham was known as a friend of God (Isa. 41:8) because of his faith. When he was old and knew his days were numbered, he sent his servant back to his country and relatives to find a wife for Isaac. When the servant got there, he had no idea where to look. So he asked God to show him by suggesting a specific response from the right girl. He had done all Abraham asked in making the trip and he didn't want to disappoint his master. Rebekah, God's choice as Isaac's wife and the answer to the servant's prayer, came on the scene even before the servant had finished praying. Not only did she have the correct response, but she was also *very beautiful* (Gen. 24:16).

The Bible has account after account of men and women of faith, Abel, Noah, Abraham and Sarah, Joshua, Esther, Daniel, Moses, and many others. So what's the point? We don't have to sweat the small (or big) stuff when we place our trust in the only One who is trustworthy, faithful, and has the power and ability to calm storms, shut the mouths of lions, and make the shadow on the steps go backward ten steps (Isa. 38:8).

How does this apply to me today? God is the same God as He was in the Old Testament. Hasn't diminished with age. He knows us by name. And He *wants* to bless us every morning (Lam. 3:22,23). But we have to do it on His terms. We have to believe that Jesus Christ is the only way to a relationship with God, that He lived, died, and was resurrected on our behalf, paying the price of our sin that we could never pay. If we have done that, then we can be assured that whatever circumstances God allows in our life are better than our best plan. But don't stop planning and working. It's been said that God will not steer a ship anchored in the harbor.

Veterans Day 2020

As a Vietnam Era veteran, I have some understanding of the commitment, the sacrifice, and the love of country the men and women who serve have as part of their character. I lost friends to this political debacle. For the most part, veterans are disciplined, respectful, and humble. Sure, there are bad apples just like everywhere else in society. But by and large I'd rather hang with guys in this group than most other groups.

Today also reminds me of the One who died in my/our place. No matter how much human blood has been or will be shed, it will never be enough to cover the sins of any let alone the entire human race.

Let the words of Paul in Romans 5:8 settle over you, *"But God demonstrates His own love toward us, in that while we were still sinners, Christ died for us."* So, veterans, thank you from the bottom of my heart for your sacrifice that allows me to live in a free country. My prayer is that you will come to know the One who sacrificed everything so we/you could live in the ultimate free country…Heaven.

October 20, 2020

God is Dangerous

Most of what we hear about God these days, if we hear anything at all, is about His love, mercy, patience, etc. But those who only present one side of God do Him a disservice. Yes, absolutely God is all those things. But if we're not told of His holiness, His wrath and intolerance of sin, and His coming judgment, we don't have the full picture and are deprived of a key motivator for preparing to meet Him. This year, our country is burning up. Record fires are burning in California and Colorado with lost lives and much destruction to property. Only a fool does not fear an out-of-control fire. Part of the picture we need to see contains words associated with God's judgment: He is a consuming fire, a flaming fire, the "anger of the Lord," destruction, destroyer. I think you get the picture.

We've become so accustomed to a slippery-slope standard, that we don't realize just how far we've fallen. Jesus had to warn the church at Ephesus with these words, "*But I have this against you, that* **you have left your first love.** *Therefore,* **remember** *from where you have fallen, and* **repent.**" Then He continued with this warning, "*or else I am coming to you and will remove your lampstand…unless you repent.*" (Rev. 2:4,5)

I am concerned that today's church—you, me, and other pew sitters—has "lost its [our] first love." Pastor Al Pittman (CWCCS.org), in a recent sermon, said this, "Show me a believer who is not growing in the Word, I'll show you someone who has no respect for God." Tough words? Yes. Needed words? Yes. Psalm 119:38 says it this way, "*Establish Your Word to Your servant as that which produces reverence for You.*" How can we respect and revere God if we're not spending time in the one thing (His Word) that shows us His heart?

What's the difference between someone asking you to do something and someone demanding it? Authority. Plug that into your view of God. God doesn't *ask* for worship and obedience from us, He *demands* it. The Liar (Satan) whispers, "tomorrow." If he can get us to postpone our worship and obedience even one day, he has succeeded. And tomorrow, he'll be back with the same whisper. Before you know it, days, or weeks have gone by and we've scarcely given God much thought. "It's OK," we tell ourselves. There's always tomorrow. We bought the lie, and we don't even realize where it came from.

It's time for the church to wake up. In Jesus' message to the church at Ephesus, He also said to the church at Sardis, "...you are dead. **Wake up...remember...repent**." (Rev. 3:1-3) That same message can be applied to us today. Time is running out. Planet earth has an expiration date. We do too.

Mere words can't say it strongly enough: WAKE UP CHURCH. As long as you have breath, God has work for you to do. There's no place in Scripture that advocates retirement. I recently heard a message where the speaker likened us (retirement age folk) to "the best wine" which, at the wedding at Cana, had been saved for last. Is that true of you and me? Do we still have a passion for the gospel of Christ? Do we recognize a lost and dying world that needs Jesus? Has *our best* been saved for last? If you can't physically be involved, you can pray. That's where the power is anyway. So don't discount it and say *all I can do* is pray. It's a key activity to move God's heart. Do it.

Thanks for reading. Check back often for more truth from God's Word.

October 23, 2020

Your Choice

Disobedience is to judgment as obedience is to blessing. In Joshua's final message to Israel, he challenged them with these words, *"If it is disagreeable in your sight to serve the Lord, choose for yourselves today whom you will serve…"* (Josh. 24:15). All of life is choices, conscious or not, we make hundreds if not thousands of them every day. Some are mundane and don't mean much, e.g. what shirt to wear. Some are significant and can carry lifelong consequences, e.g. who to marry, what career to pursue, etc.

There is *one choice* that has not only **lifelong** ramifications, but **eternal** ones as well. And that is how you answer the question, "What will I do with Jesus Christ?" If we think about today's opening line, I don't think any of us would consciously choose judgment over blessing. But here's the thing. Obedience *has* to be a conscious decision. Otherwise, left to "chance," our default is *always* disobedience. Without conscious choice, we're by nature lazy and undisciplined. We have to choose to get up and go to work, choose to wash the dishes, etc. You get the point.

Whichever way you answer The Question, the consequences are eternal. Putting it off, by default, results in judgment. So what, you say? I don't believe in all that stuff, you say. OK. Maybe you don't believe in the law of sowing and reaping either. In today's vernacular, "what goes around, comes around." It's your choice. But imagine yourself as the rich man (we'll call him Bob) in Jesus' parable of Bob and Lazarus in Luke 16:19-31. They both die. Lazarus goes to heaven (Abraham's bosom) and Bob is buried and shows up in Hades (precursor to hell). Listen to Bob's tormented plea, *"Father Abraham,* **have mercy on me**, *and send Lazarus so that he may dip the tip of his finger in water and cool off my tongue, for* **I am in agony in this flame.**" (v.24) Notice, their spirits are both *still alive*. There *is* life after death. There are only *two* destinations.

Bob asks for mercy. Three things are wrong with that request. First, he's asking the wrong person. Only Jesus can grant mercy. Second, his motive is wrong. All he wants is to ease his suffering, he's not sorry for the wrong choices, he's only sorry he got caught. Third, it's too late. The Bible says, "*It is appointed for men to die once, and after this comes judgment*" (Heb. 9:27). There is no place in the Bible that describes Purgatory or any other intermediate place after death. You either go to heaven to be with Jesus forever, or you're in hell suffering like Bob...forever. No second chance after you die.

Harsh words? Maybe. But if you're heading for a cliff and there's no guardrail, don't you appreciate a "danger ahead" alert? God is a God of love "*who desires all men to be saved and to come to the knowledge of the truth.*" (1 Tim. 2:4), but He doesn't force anyone. Consider this *your* "danger ahead alert". And don't wait. Time is running out when it will be too late.

October 25, 2020

No Means No

Many of us have trained our kids to wait for the 3rd or 4th "no" before they even act like we've spoken. When my kids were little, we were taught and practiced the concept of "first time obedience," say it once and if they don't obey—boom (whatever the appropriate discipline). I got tired of threatening. And this new concept worked most of the time.

You know it's almost funny when I think about some of the implied threats I've heard and maybe used some myself. Things like, "don't make me come in there" or "wait 'til your father gets home." They all have one thing in common. They teach our little ones that we don't mean what we say…until we get mad and raise our voice. Anybody relate to that?

I was reading in Joshua this morning. Moses had just died. Joshua was in charge of the Israelite mob. His task was to go to war with all the surrounding people and kill everything that moved men, women, animals, everything. Whatever spoil was taken was for the treasury of the Lord. Nothing was to be taken for personal use. God fought their battles for them and defeated ALL their enemies…up until now. Enter Achan. He obviously didn't take Joshua's warning from God seriously. Must have been a 3rd or 4th time kid growing up. He took some of the spoils from Jericho for himself and hid them in his tent. Nobody knew.

The next battle was at Ai, a comparatively small town. Joshua led only a portion of his army (about 3,000 men) out to battle the little group, because his spies had reported back that, "they are few." But the men of Ai routed Joshua's army and killed three dozen of his soldiers. Joshua sought the Lord as to why He had let this happen.

As usual, God got right to the point with Joshua. He said, "Israel has sinned…taken…things under the ban and have stolen and deceived." (Jos. 7:11) You can read the whole narrative in Joshua 7 and 8. Spoiler alert: The end of the story is that God ultimately gave them the win over Ai **after** they dealt with Achan. It didn't turn out so well for Achan. Joshua took Achan, his sons, daughters, oxen, donkeys, sheep, all he'd stolen, and all that belonged to him and stoned them and burned them. Boom.

All justice belongs to God. That should be a comfort to us who know Him. It should scare the pants off those who don't. Nobody but nobody gets away with sin. It may seem like it sometimes when those who have wronged us skate. But if we don't know the forgiveness of sin paid for by Jesus Christ, this world is as good as it gets. The next is horrible. But for those of us in Christ, our sins are forgiven, our debt fully paid, and our home in paradise awaits.

When you stand in judgment and ask God to let you into heaven, know Jesus and the answer is yes. No Jesus and no means no. It's not too late to confess your sin and move to the yes line. Find out how by turning to the Appendix *Steps to Salvation.*

October 26, 2020

No God No Heaven No Hurry

All three are lies from the pit. One has greater success than the others. The devil can't get most people to outright believe there is no God or no heaven. But "no hurry," that's a winner. "There's always tomorrow," he says. And like the people who mocked Peter's message about Christ's return, (*"Where's the promise of His coming? For ever since the fathers fell asleep, all continues just as it was from the beginning of creation."* [2 Pet. 3:4]), today's mockers swallow the lie and blow off the warnings too. Many have twisted the age-old adage to fit their bent to procrastination, "never do today what you can put off until tomorrow."

There's also a twist (lie) on the existence of heaven. Jesus talks about two ways (narrow and broad) in Matthew 7:13,14. The devil doesn't deny the existence of heaven, he just changes the road sign and labels the road to hell, heaven. The narrow way (the right path to heaven) doesn't appeal to the masses. There are rules to obey, shiny objects to reject, delayed gratification to practice. The broad way (the path to hell) has none of those silly restrictions. Great mass appeal. That's why Jesus says of the narrow way, *"there are few who find it."* (Matt. 7:14)

Why do many reject the warnings of Christ's return for His church? I think it's like the neighbor's car alarm that is overly sensitive and goes off all the time. We eventually tune it out. There had never been a worldwide flood…until there was. God destroyed the entire earth except for 8 people and the animals Noah brought into the ark. At a minimum, those who perished had at least 100 years of warning. That's how long it took Noah to build the ark. Today, we've had millennia to consider the warnings. But just like the car alarm, we've tuned them out.

I believe the deeper issue is we just don't want accountability. Well, here's the hard truth. We either deal with our sins **before** we die and face God as one of His children, loved and forgiven, or we face Him **after** we die as our righteous judge and jailer.

How many of you have experienced the sudden death of a friend or loved one? We often hear, "before his time" when it's a child or younger person. But that's not true. The Bible tells us that each of us has an expiration date (Ps. 139:16) ordained by God before we were born. I know from personal experience that tomorrow is not guaranteed; I have buried two children (1-yr old, 27-yr old).

My purpose in writing is not to condemn you, your sins have already done that. No, it's to be a beacon in a dark place pointing you to the safety of a relationship with Jesus Christ. Someone said that a lighthouse is only a tourist attraction…until it gets dark. Are you in a dark place today? Heed the alarms, don't tune them out. Come to the Savior before it's too late. Check out our "Steps to Salvation" Appendix.

October 31, 2020

Stinky Sponges

What do sponges do? They soak up whatever they come in contact with. They are used to clean up messes, to wipe away dirt and grime. If not rinsed and squeezed out, they become stinky. And if not used frequently, they become hard and unusable for their intended purpose. My wife occasionally will wet one and nuke it to kill any bacteria.

We are a lot like sponges. We absorb what we come in contact with e.g. music, styles, slang, opinions, etc. And, like sponges, if we're exposed to worldly trends and not occasionally flushed and squeezed out by the Holy Spirit and the Word of God, we become stinky too. If we're not in the Word daily, we can become hardened to the things of God and unusable for God's purposes.

In a recent article published by Family Research Council President, Tony Perkins, titled *"Latest Surveys Show a Worldview of Differences,"* George Barna, who directs the Cultural Research Center at Arizona Christian University, says, *"Only **six percent** of adults in this country have a 'Biblical worldview.'"* Perkins calls it *"a shocker of a statistic that has more Christians wondering what on earth are parents and churches teaching?"*

Sponges. Soaking up the wrong stuff. How do we avoid that when we're immersed in a sin-cursed world day in and day out? As always, the Bible has the answer. We are told to *"be filled with the Spirit"* (Eph. 5:18) and *"walk by the Spirit and you will not carry out the desire of the flesh."* (Gal. 5:16)

You don't have to look very far today to see the devastating effects of a non-Biblical worldview. Paul wrote about it two millennia ago (2 Tim. 3:1-5; emphasis added) *"...**in the last days** difficult times will come. For men will be lovers of self, lovers of money, boastful, arrogant, revilers, disobedient to parents, ungrateful, unholy, unloving, irreconcilable, malicious gossips, without self-control, brutal, haters of good, treacherous, reckless, conceited, lovers of pleasure rather than lovers of God, holding to a form of godliness, although they have denied its power. **Avoid such men as these.**"* I think that just about covers society today in America.

Does that mean we're in the last days? We have been since Jesus' first visit to earth. Does it mean we're in the last of the last days? I don't know, but it sure feels like it. This book is filled with the good news that Jesus Christ died in our place so that we could live in His place (heaven). If you *know* where you'll spend eternity, then make sure you're filled and walking in the Spirit. If you *don't know* where you'll spend eternity, please spend a few minutes in our "Steps to Salvation" Appendix.

Thanks for reading.

November 3, 2020

Who do you look like?

Remember the fun-house mirrors in amusement parks of days gone by? We could look taller, fatter, have different proportions. According to the American Society of Plastic Surgeons, Americans spent over $16.5 billion in 2018 to change the way they looked. With over 8,000 member surgeons, that's somewhere around $2 million for each. I'm in the wrong business.

Why are we so willing to spend out-of-pocket dollars on that elusive goal of eternal youth? Simple. We've made beauty a god. I can understand that. With some exceptions, there aren't many ugly people on the big screen or in spokesperson ads. I don't know what the Apostle Paul looked like, but I do know his character. It was one of being totally sold out for Jesus. And that's why he can say, *"Be imitators of me, just as I also am of Christ."* (1 Cor. 11:1)

What would it take to shift our focus from how we look to how we act? The most important element would be to have the right role model. There are so many to choose from today. Movie stars. Sports figures. And, heaven forbid, politicians. Why can Paul say that we should imitate him? Because he sets the bar for who to imitate. Before you choose anybody to copy, ask yourself this: "If I follow them all the way, where do I end up? Are they on the wide or narrow path that Jesus described? (Matt. 7:13,14)"

Do *you* know what path you're on? Have you considered the consequences of the wrong path? They are both labeled "heaven." But only one is correct. The wide path, with many on it, is filled with shiny objects—things that distract us from the fact we're on the wrong path. What's *your* plan to get to the end? It's been said that if you fail to plan, you plan to fail. One of the biggest enemies of planning and thinking about our future is noise. Look around. Almost everybody has something plugged into their ears. Constant noise doesn't allow us to think, to meditate, to silently praise God for another day.

When you look in the mirror of God's Word, do you like what you see? If you're a sinner saved by grace and faith in Jesus Christ, then in spite of your warts and (perceived) flaws, God sees you as perfect. By the way, His is the only standard that matters. No standard the world compares you to has any validity. Iconic vocalist, Ethel Waters (1896-1977), coined the phrase, "I am somebody cause God don't make no junk!"

If you're being pulled by the sirens of society to a path you feel is wrong and you want to shift your focus from "look" to "act," visit our *Steps to Salvation* Appendix. It lays out a step-by-step plan that clearly shows the ONLY way to a permanent relationship with the God who loves you and His Son, Jesus Christ. Thanks for reading.

November 8, 2020

How Does Your Garden Grow?

I have to tell you neither of my thumbs is green. But this year my wife talked me into helping her plant tomatoes, carrots, and cucumbers, two of the three I don't eat. I'm sure I'll be rewarded in heaven. Of course the tomatoes did fine. But as soon as the carrots began to sprout, rabbits ate all the green tops. Don't know what happened to the cukes, the vines grew but never had a crop.

My morning reading took me through 1 Corinthians this week where I was reminded that, "…*neither the one who plants nor the one who waters is anything, but God who causes the growth.*" (1 Cor. 3:7) I know this doesn't refer to literal gardens, but the principle is still true. All I can say is God must like tomatoes better than cukes and carrots.

What does this have to do with being a follower of Jesus Christ? Just like God causes the growth in our gardens, He is the One responsible for growth in His church. This verse should be a real encouragement to any who want to share the gospel (plant/water) but are hesitant because of lack of knowledge, lack of courage, or lack of faith. The good news of this verse is that *we're not responsible* for the results (others turning to Christ), just the faithfulness of opening our mouth and spreading the truth of God's Word. Here's another encouragement, "*My Word…will not return to Me empty…without succeeding in the matter for which I sent it.*" (Isa. 55:11)

My career was largely in the sales arena where the *only thing* one is measured on is results. Some of the principles of successful selling are the same for witnessing. One of the biggest mistakes salesmen make is they never *ask for the order.*

After sharing Christ, however you do that using a tool like Evangelism Explosion, the Romans Road, the Way of the Master, or just telling your own story of coming to Christ, asking a question like, "Does this make sense to you?" or "Would you like to give your life to Christ right now?" can gently prod for a decision. If they say yes, lead them in a prayer of confession and submission (see sample in *Steps to Salvation* Appendix). The precise words are not important. The attitude of the heart is. If they say no, ask clarifying questions such as, "Is there some particular point you don't understand?" or "Is there anything I can answer for you?" Don't badger. The Holy Spirit is at work and only He knows their heart.

The world measures us by their standard of success. But the ONLY standard we should concern ourselves with is the one God set out in His Word, one of **obedience** to Him, **faithfulness** to Him, *"preach the word, be ready in season and out of season" (1 Tim. 4:2)*, *"be ready to make a defense...for the hope that is in you"* (1 Pet.3:15). Both of these verses add either "with gentleness and reverence" or "with great patience and instruction." Proverbs 16:21 tells us, *"...sweetness of speech increases persuasiveness."* When people are confronted with their sin, they may not react as you'd like. Remember Jesus was "gentle and humble in heart" (Matt.11:29). That's our example of how to plant and water. Go and do likewise. Thanks for reading

December 2, 2020

I Am—You're Not

Pride is ugly and insidious. It's a liar. It says I'm all that and a bag of chips, when in truth, everything I have was *given* to me (I Cor. 4:7) and "…apart from Me [Jesus] you [I] can do nothing." (John 15:5)

We get degrees and more degrees, we buy things and more things, we join clubs, we want to be seen as successful. And maybe we are, according to the world's standard. My question is, So what? God's Word tells us all that "stuff" will burn up. Jesus also warns those of us who are lukewarm towards Him, "…*I will spit you out of My mouth. Because you say, 'I am rich, and have become wealthy, and have need of nothing.' and you do not know that you are wretched and miserable and poor and blind and naked.*" (Rev. 3:16,17)

John 15 tells us about vines and branches. Jesus says **"I am** the true vine," the implication is that we're not. We want to be the vine. We want credit for fruit produced by the vine. That's our pride lying to us again. We are branches. Branches are dependent on the vine for nourishment and fruit. A branch can only produce fruit of the type initiated by the vine. If we want to produce fruit—which will have eternal rewards—the first step is to make sure we're *abiding* in the Vine. We do that by having a personal relationship with God through His Son, Jesus Christ. Then we spend time in God's Word…daily. If we do that, the fruit will be a byproduct that comes naturally.

Jesus also warns if we don't abide in Him, we are "*thrown away…and cast into the fire*" (John 15:6) That's the result of believing pride's lie. Sin always promises good, fun, sexy, but only delivers death. It says, "nobody will know" or "you deserve it" or "you can stop anytime." But the Bible says, "*Come out from their midst and be separate, says the Lord. And do not touch what is unclean; and I will welcome you.*" (2 Cor. 6:17)

As the season in which we celebrate the birth of our Lord Jesus Christ approaches, let's remember that it's not about sparkly trees and shiny-wrapped gifts under them but about THE gift that came humbly as a baby destined for a painful death so that we could live. If you haven't received *that* gift yet, visit our *Steps to Salvation* Appendix for a clear picture of your future.

December 10, 2020

Turn on the Light

Little kids are often afraid of the dark and some never outgrow it. Most homes have a form of nightlight to combat the dark. The boogeyman checks under his bed for Chuck Norris. At camp, we sit 'round the campfire telling spooky stories…just before bedtime. Nyctophobia is fairly common—a severe fear of the dark—and with good cause. Bad things happen in the dark.

There is a category of people that love the dark: "…*and men loved the darkness rather than the Light, for their deeds were evil. For everyone who does evil hates the Light, and does not come to the Light for fear that his deeds will be exposed.*" (John 3:19,20) During the runup to our recent presidential election, we heard a lot about transparency in government. Based on the verse above, that's not likely to happen. The good news is that deliverance for us individually, as a nation, and even the entire world is NOT from any form of government but ONLY through our Lord Jesus Christ.

For those who have nothing to hide, transparency is a good thing. As Jesus was about to be introduced to Nathaniel, He said, "*an Israelite indeed, in whom there is no deceit.*" (John 1:47) What did He mean? Simply that Nathaniel's bluntness was an indication he had no deceptive motives.

As people heading for one of two eternal destinations, we need more than a dim nightlight. We need the Light (capital L) of the world to escape permanent darkness. Jesus said, "*I am the Light of the world, he who follows me will not walk in the darkness.*" (John 8:12)

Tired of living in the darkness of sin? There's only one way out. It's time to turn on the light, to come to the Light. Jesus said, "*the one who comes to Me I will certainly not cast out.*" (John 6:37) Morality is spinning out of control and in danger of disappearing altogether. Lawlessness is rampant. The "me" generation has exploded on the scene with destruction in their path.

Time is running out. Choose Christ while you still have breath. Contrary to what some religions teach, there is no second chance. The Bible says, "*It is appointed for men to die once, and after this comes judgment.*" (Heb. 9:27) If you'd like to know more, visit our *Steps to*

Salvation Appendix. Do it now. The devil's biggest lie is, "there's always tomorrow." Not true. Each of us has an expiration date assigned by God the Creator before we were born. (Ps. 139:16) Stay in the dark and you're bound to stumble over something..

December 16, 2020

Growth, Not Perfection

Military slogans abound. "Be all you can be", "A few good men", and others. And they are good in their intent. They just miss the mark of eternal significance. Ask yourself, "What is the goal of a slogan?" Isn't it something to motivate you toward a defined end? There's nothing wrong, in and of themselves, with slogans. But without eternal focus, it's a case of the good getting in the way of the best.

Today's thought comes from a verse in John, "*He must increase, but I must decrease*" (3:30). Scripture says, "*...be perfect, as your heavenly Father is perfect*" (Matt.5:48). *Positionally*, because of Jesus' death on our behalf, we already are perfect. But *practically* we won't see it in our earthly bodies. Paul tells us why, "*For I know that nothing good dwells in me, that is, in my flesh, for the willing [to do good] is present in me, but the doing of the good is not*" (Rom. 7:18).

So, let's call our title—Growth, Not Perfection—our slogan. And rather than adopt it for a specific length of time, e.g. our enlistment period, can we make it a life goal? If we look at today's verse, it almost seems the antithesis of our slogan. On one hand, we are to grow. On the other we are to decrease. How's that work? Remember, we march to a different drummer. We have a different standard than the world. Often the two standards are exact opposites. The world tells us to "go for the gusto." The Bible tells us, "*humility goes before honor*" (Prov. 18:12). The world tells us "you have to look out for number one." The Bible tells us, "*...with humility of mind regard one another as more important than yourselves*" (Phil. 2:3).

I didn't say it was going to be easy. But then nothing that lasts into eternity is. All our lives we've been bombarded with the world's ways, the world's standards of right and wrong. How's that working out for the world? Just take 2020 as our example. Hatred, lying, and self-promotion have had disastrous results all across our country.

As you consider how to apply our slogan and verse, I leave you with these encouraging words from Jesus shortly before His crucifixion, "*...in Me you may have peace. In the world you have tribulation, but take courage; I have overcome the world*" (John 16:33). Are you growing or just marking time?

December 25, 2020

Today is Christmas

We've all heard the Christmas story about how God became man in the form of a baby with the sole purpose of dying on the cross to redeem sinful man. Have you ever really considered why? Why would God, who is self-existent and needs nothing, bother creating mankind, knowing how depraved we'd become to the point of rejecting His love demonstrated by His son, Jesus Christ, and murdering Him in the most painful way practiced by man in that day?

I believe we have a very limited view of God. We've been told of His anger, wrath, and judgment of sin. We sin. So we fear His punishment. And rightfully so because it's forever. But let's look at it a different way. Let's look at what God is and what He offers to those who believe in Jesus.

God is holy. Because we've never known a world without sin, it's hard to grasp what that means. We're so used to a world where self-absorption, arrogance, and debauchery are the norm that we can't picture life without it. And many of today's churches do a poor job of painting a true picture of God.

So, why are we here? God's splendor, majesty, creative power is awesome and because of God's character of love, mercy, grace, forgiveness, generosity and much more, He wants to bless us with the results of all that. The prophet Jeremiah tells us in Lamentations 3:22,23, "*The Lord's lovingkindnesses indeed never cease. For His compassions never fail. They are new every morning. Great is your faithfulness.*" Can we get our arms around a God who just wants to share Himself with us for no other reason than He loves us?

Some will say that God is narcissistic and needs approval or reinforcement from man. Couldn't be farther from the truth. His love is unconditional, ever giving, pure, and we can't comprehend that because it's not how we love. He has created heaven **for us** to enjoy…forever. Jesus told us, "*I go to prepare a place for you. If I go and prepare a place for you, I **will come again** and receive you to Myself, that where I am, there you may be also.*" (John 14:2,3). Why would you want to spend eternity with someone you don't know very well? How do we get to know Him? The Bible is the best tool we have.

The Psalmist asks God to, "...*establish Your word to Your servant as that which produces reverence for You.*" Ps. 119:38.

We view God's righteous anger over sin incorrectly when we only think of God as the punisher. His motive is not to punish, it's to restore us to fellowship with Him **so that** we don't miss out on anything He has planned for our future. What a promise. What a gift...the best possible way to celebrate Christmas. Have you received the gift yet? It's available to all who believe in the Lord Jesus Christ as *the only* way to a restored relationship with the only One who loves us unconditionally, the only One who paid the price for sin that we could not pay. The only One who not only wants us to spend eternity with Him but who took care of all the details and preparation to get ready for our arrival. If you're not sure your spot has been reserved, check out our "*Steps to Salvation*" Appendix in the back of this book.

Thanks for stopping by. Hope to see you on the other side.

December 31, 2020

The Last Day(s)

Twenty-twenty has finally come to an end. And if that meant a new beginning, I'd be celebrating. Alas, the horizon is dark with foreboding signs not of politics as usual, but politics worse than ever. But I have good news…and bad news.

The bad news is man's heart is *"more deceitful than all else and is desperately sick"* (Jer.17:9). It hasn't gotten better in the approximately 2,700 years since Jeremiah's writing. In fact, it's been that way a lot longer.

Before the worldwide flood described in Genesis 6 & 7, God's take was, *"the wickedness of man was great on the earth, and that every intent of the thoughts of his heart was only evil continually"* (Gen. 6:5). Boom. Then it started to rain. You know the rest of the story. Everyone on earth except for 8 people—*"but Noah found favor in the eyes of the Lord"*—were destroyed in the flood.

The fact that man's heart is predisposed to wickedness makes him a prime target for the lies of the devil, the destroyer, Satan himself. When God created the earth in six days, he *"saw all that He had made, and behold, it was **very** good…and He rested on the seventh day"* (Gen. 1:31-2:2).

So it started out "very good." But the devil hates God and for over 6,000 years has done everything he can to corrupt the creation with lies, deception, innuendo, and his favorite, the forbidden fruit. Look around at the world in 2020. Can you find anything anywhere that is getting morally better, more peaceful, or more hopeful? My guess is, no you can't. It's the second law of thermodynamics at work (order moves to chaos).

But I promised good news. As bad as the world is today, it's all part of God's plan to redeem sinful man and place him in a new heaven and new earth where the perfection of original creation reigns forever. Why would God do that? To answer that, you have to know something about Him, the one true God, to understand His motives.

God is love. He doesn't just love, He *IS* love. A love we can't comprehend because of our wicked hearts. Our love is conditional. You love me, I'll love you. You do for me, I'll do for you. Not God.

"*For God so loved the world, that He gave his only Son* [Jesus] *that whoever believes in Him will not perish but have everlasting life.*" (John 3:16) That is a powerful statement about His character. But listen to this one, "*While we were still helpless, at the right time Christ died for the ungodly...God demonstrates His own love toward us, in that while we were yet sinners, Christ died for us*" (Rom. 5:6,8).

Sin separates us from a loving Father. We sin and don't want anything to do with God because He demands we come to Him on His terms, i.e. believe that Jesus Christ paid the penalty for our sin so that we could be restored to a loving relationship with God through Christ. So, back to the question, why would God do that? Because He loves us and has prepared an amazing home for us with Him. He doesn't want us to miss out because we've bought Satan's shiny package of lies, distractions and anything he can use to keep us from the only One in the universe who loves us unconditionally. Heaven will be phenomenal. You don't want to miss it.

This entire book is committed to sounding the alarm that Jesus is coming back. With all the worldwide signs of debauchery and our gathering speed down the slippery slope of "too late," it could be very soon. In addition to the warning, we also lay out the way to be sure you're not left behind. Visit our "*Steps to Salvation*" Appendix for all the details. Hope to see you there.

The Time of Our Life

A second, a minute, an hour
Does not diminish God's power
He's the same today[1]
No less any way
We hide in the strength of His tower.[2]

A minute, an hour a day
What more are we able to say
Than God's on His throne[3]
We're never alone[4]
He bids us all come and pray.[5]

An hour, a day, or a week
We ask, and we knock, and we seek[6]
The world, we are told
Is not for the bold
It belongs to those who are meek.[7]

A day, or a week or a year
Our Father could not be more near[8]
He plans our reward[9]
To know Him as Lord[10]
If we're quiet, His voice we will hear.

A week or a year or our life
Whether filled with darkness and strife
Can never compare
To what we'll hear there
"Welcome home" my bride and my wife.[11]

Mike Thornton

[1] Heb. 13:8
[2] Prov. 18:10
[3] Psa. 11:4
[4] Deut. 31:8
[5] Psa. 105:4
[6] Matt. 7:7
[7] Matt. 5:5
[8] Psa. 145:18
[9] Isa. 40:10
[10] Phil. 3:10
[11] Luke 19:17; Rev. 19:7

January 1, 2021

Leave God Out…at your own peril

As I look back over the past 12 months, several things stand out. But I think the most dramatic is how confidence in our political and scientific leaders has all but evaporated. It's like the old joke about how you know when a lawyer (politician, scientist, etc.) is lying…his lips are moving. Not so funny anymore.

The landscape is littered with lies, half-truths, innuendo, all supported and promoted by the media whose job was supposed to be to hold those in authority accountable. Hatred has replaced objectivity as the measuring stick by which decisions are made. Hidden agendas, possibly driven by greed and kept from wondering eyes, have spawned conspiracy theories galore.

Freedoms, heretofore taken for granted, have been slashed by power-hungry (little "g") gods looking for their 15 minutes of fame while destroying lives, businesses, and our robust economy in general. All means of social interaction—schools, churches, restaurants, etc.— have been virtually eliminated in the name of flattening the curve. "Science" was thought to have all the answers. Only problem, they kept changing the answers.

But that was 2020. This is 2021. Whether you believe in the God of the Bible or not, He WILL have His way. The Bible warns us, *"Why are the nations in an uproar and the peoples devising a vain thing? The kings of the earth take their stand and the rulers take counsel together against the Lord and against His anointed, saying, 'Let us tear their fetters apart and cast away their cords from us!' **He who sits in the heavens laughs, the Lord scoffs at them. Then He will speak to them in His anger and terrify them in His fury.**"* (Psalm 2:1-5).

Not believing in God is like not believing in the law of gravity. It doesn't matter what you believe, that law cannot be broken. And just because you don't believe in or want accountability to the One that you *will* stand before in judgment someday, doesn't change the reality. The Bible also says, *"For **the wrath of God** is revealed from heaven **against all ungodliness and unrighteousness of men who suppress the truth** in unrighteousness, because **that which is known about God*** *is evident within them; for God made it evident to them…so that they are without excuse.*" (Rom. 1:18-20)

Without excuse means just that. No amount of blaming others or circumstances will carry any weight in God's courtroom. But, and here's the unbelievably good news, there is ONE WAY to "beat the rap." In spite of all the "ungodliness and unrighteousness" hurled at God in ignorance and arrogance, He still loves us with unconditional love; love not based on what we do or don't do but love based on God's character alone. *"For God so loved the world that He gave His only Son [Jesus Christ], that whoever believes in Him will not perish but will have eternal life."* (John 3:16)

What does it mean to "believe in Jesus?" God is holy and cannot tolerate sin. We sin. As a result, the relationship God wants to have with us has been broken. Jesus came to earth specifically to pay the debt our sin created and which we could never pay with good deeds or any amount of money. So what's the catch? No catch, we just have to do it God's way. And that's where many will miss the train. Our pride cannot admit we've been wrong about God and allow us to turn from our wicked ways and trust Jesus' "paid in full" pardon. That's the gist of today's title. It's a life and death decision…literally.

I would like to think you've read this far because God is calling you to Himself, not to a religion, not to a set of laws and regulations, but to the magnificent grace and mercy He offers everyone. He wants a relationship with you and has created an eternal home in heaven where NONE of the sin which has led to 2020 will exist…ever. If you'd like to know more about this God, check out our *"Steps to Salvation"* appendix in the back of this book.

Thanks for reading. If you have questions, contact us. We'd love to hear from you.

February 16, 2021

Ready or Not…

O.T. prophet Ezekiel lived about 600 years before Christ. He had the privilege (?) of passing along God's message of condemnation to the people of Israel. As I read this morning in chapters 6-7 of Ezekiel's prophecy, I couldn't help feeling that this message could have just as easily been for today. Listen to some of his warnings: (God speaking) *"I have been hurt by their adulterous hearts which turned away from me…I have not said in vain that I would inflict this disaster on them…thus I will spend My wrath on them. Then you will know that I am the Lord when their slain are among their idols."*

God's patience was at an end with his "chosen" people, Israel. They continually whined to Him when things weren't going well. As soon as He delivered them, they were right back to their adulterous ways. (Not a sexual reference, but idolatry.) They had plenty of warnings. Six times in two chapters, God describes the wrath and anger He is about to pour out on them and then says, *"then they will know that I am the Lord."* They ignored them all. Oops.

As a rule, we don't worship gold, silver, and wooden idols today. No, our idols are more subtle. It's more likely our idols are money (which could include gold and silver), power, position, fancy houses, and even ourselves. Literally anything that takes God's place on the throne is an idol.

Hindsight is always 20/20. And we can look back over 2,500 years and see the destruction of Jerusalem and ask why Israel didn't heed the warnings. But aren't we in the exact same position? We lie and don't think anything of it. We murder babies in the womb by the millions. And now even after they've left the womb, they're not safe. Our streets are not safe from violent gangs. As we saw last summer, certain politicians have no will or desire to stand up against their burning, looting, and destruction of lives and property.

But you know, we've had our warnings from God too. And, like the Israelites, we don't pay any attention. This example in Ezekiel is not the only case of God's patience running out. There are more. The point I'm making is this, God's ways are clear. First, He warns and warns and warns. Then He acts, and people are surprised when He does exactly what He said He would do.

Listen to some of the descriptions and see if it doesn't play like today's newspaper. *"But realize this, that in the **last days** difficult times will come. For men will be lovers of self, lovers of money, boastful, arrogant, revilers, disobedient to parents, ungrateful, unholy, unloving, irreconcilable, malicious gossips, without self-control, brutal, haters of good, treacherous, reckless, conceited, lovers of pleasure rather than lovers of God, holding to a form of godliness, although they have denied its power; Avoid such men as these."* (2 Tim. 3:1-5)

We've had over 2,000 years of warnings about Christ's return to earth for His church—those who believe He died on the cross in their place, then rose from the dead. He is now in heaven until "the time" runs out. We *are* running out of time. We'll also run out of excuses. God's Word is crystal clear as to **what** will happen, just not exactly **when** it will happen. Someday, soon I hope, millions of Christians all over the world will suddenly disappear. It's because Jesus has returned and taken us to heaven. You may have heard of it. It's called the Rapture. Only those who have a personal relationship with Jesus Christ are included.

For me and all who know Jesus as their Savior, this is an exciting time thinking Jesus may return in our lifetime. For those who have rejected Jesus, the plagues predicted in Revelation 6-19 (all 21 of them) should scare the pants off you. Know this: God's Word is always 100% accurate. Just like He told the Israelites 2,500 years ago what He was planning, and then He did it, He has told us specifically what He is planning. It will happen. If you're one who continues to deny and disregard the warnings, you're in for the worst seven years you can possibly imagine starting immediately after the Rapture. Then you die and will know firsthand what hell is like. If you're reading this, it's not too late to choose Jesus.

If anything in this post strikes a chord, you can visit our *Steps to Salvation* Appendix in the back of this book. Or you can get in touch via email. My prayer is that everyone who reads this either already knows Jesus or gets introduced soon. Tomorrow isn't promised to anybody.

February 21, 2021

Nothing to See Here

Cover ups. Fake news. Lies. "Nothing to see here" is the common don't-look-too-deep phrase that is intended to keep us moving. I'm still in Ezekiel and almost had to laugh at how timely God's prophet's message to the false prophets of his day is for the false prophets of our day. In chapter 13, verse 3, God says, *"Woe to the foolish prophets who are following their own spirit and have seen nothing* [from God]." I'm talking about the false prophets of climate change, mask efficacy, peace through negotiations, evolution vs. creation, and it goes on.

But here's the scary part. Their message resonates with a large part of our population. Why? I believe there are a number of reasons, but I'll limit it to three. First and foremost, they don't know the Bible or the God of the Bible because they reject accountability to Him. Second, their lives are focused on the "shiny objects" offered by the world instead of having an eternal perspective on anything. All their efforts go into getting and having, not realizing that it will all burn up someday. Never seen a hearse towing a U-Haul. Third, it's easy to believe a lie that doesn't challenge our lethargy or demand anything more than blind obedience to the current "talking points" of the "experts."

What's my point? I'm just a guy who loves Jesus and knows what the Bible says about the future. In chapters 6-17 of Ezekiel, sixteen times, God says some form of, *"so that they will know that I am the Lord."* What was He referring to? A literal and detailed description of the judgments He would pour out on the Israelites. Did it happen the way He said it would? Every last detail.

Why is that important? Two reasons. First, God knows before it happens because He controls the future. Second, it proves His Word, the Bible, is true. So what? Only that He has told us **exactly** what He plans to do with the world and the people in it when the final bell rings. Not counting the Old Testament prophets who foretold our future, we've had over two millennia since Jesus Christ walked the earth to hear the warnings of coming doom and to be ready. We've had increasing signs of the imminency of Christ's return to take His Church home to heaven.

It's true that every generation has felt the same, that Jesus would return in their lifetime. But what's different now? One of the biggest-impact prophesies about the last days was fulfilled in May 1948 when Israel became a nation again. People didn't believe Noah's warnings about pending disaster either when he was building a big boat for over 100 years before the flood. There had never been a flood…until there was. The Apostle Peter nails it, *"Know this first of all, that in the last days mockers will come with their mocking, following after their own lusts, and saying, 'Where is the promise of His coming? For ever since the fathers fell asleep, all continues just as it was from the beginning of creation."* (2 Peter 3:3,4)…and then the rain started.

A one-world government, one-world currency, a mark without which you can't buy or sell, all seemed far-fetched only a few years ago. Not so far off now, is it, with all the controls relating to COVID-19 in place?

Last post we talked about the 21 plagues described in Revelation 6-19. They happen during a 7-year period called The Tribulation. They happen *after* Christ takes His people to heaven, and *before* the final judgment. There will be no more warnings as to exactly when this will happen. We must be ready. The Bible says, *"If the head of the house had known at what time of the night the thief was coming, he would have been on the alert and would not have allowed his house to be broken into."* (Matt. 24:43). This is talking about Christ's return (the Rapture). No warning. No time to pack a go-bag. For those of us who have trusted Jesus Christ for forgiveness of our sins, we eagerly antic-ipate His return. For those who haven't, there's still time…just not much.

The good news is that God loves you in spite of your rejection, your denials, your sin. But you have to come to Him on His terms, not yours. Good deeds won't get you in. Church attendance won't get you in. Only your acceptance of Christ's death on the cross *as your substi-tute* will get you into heaven. Trust me. Heaven is where you want to spend eternity, not hell. Heaven is glorious, no sin, no lying, no pain. We're in Christ's presence forever. Hell is "weeping and gnashing of teeth" in utter darkness. Right now, the choice is still yours. See *Steps to Salvation* for more details.

February 23, 2021

Get FAT not fatter

Faithfulness, Availability, and Teachable are the focus of our talk today.

In the book, *Christ in Men...Today*, we see these character qualities in detail. This will be just a 30,000 ft. view.

Can we agree that character counts? Society at large doesn't seem to think so anymore. Signs of slippage are everywhere especially in the political arena—both sides. But we march to a different drummer. Our commanding officer hasn't, nor will He ever, change our orders. Christ is our character model. Scripture gives us a thorough picture of God's faithfulness. A favorite verse is Lamentations 3:22-24, *"The Lord's lovingkindnesses indeed never cease, for His compassions **never fail**. They are new every morning; **great is Your faithfulness**. 'The Lord is my portion,' says my soul, 'therefore I have hope in Him.'"*

Proverbs 27:6 tells us, *"Faithful are the wounds of a friend, but deceitful are the kisses of an enemy."* What does that mean? Only true friends, those who love us enough to tell us the truth even when it hurts, are worthy to be called "friend." Some will tell lies to flatter or con us into some action that will benefit **them** and not necessarily **us**. Jesus told His church in Smyrna, *"...be faithful unto death and I will give you the crown of life."* (Rev. 2:10). Faithfulness benefits us now by being a true friend and also when Christ comes with His reward. (Rev. 22:12).

It's been said that the only ability God looks for is "avail-ability." God told Jeremiah, *"Roam the streets of Jerusalem... If you can find a man... if there is one who does justice...then I will pardon her* [Israel]" (Jer. 5:1). *"Then I* [Isaiah] *heard the voice of the Lord, saying, 'Whom shall I send, and who will go for Us?' Then I said, 'Here am I. Send me.!'"* (Isa. 6:8). Ask most pastors, "Who does most of the ministry at your church?" He'll likely answer the same 20% over and over. Jesus told His disciples, *"The harvest is plentiful, but the laborers are few; therefore beseech the Lord of the harvest to send out laborers into His harvest."* (Luke 10:2).

Why does God have such a hard time finding volunteers? Is it because the pastor gets paid and we think, "it's not my job?" Or could it be we don't have Christ's heart for the lost? Might it be we don't feel "qualified" to share the gospel? May I remind us that it's *not by might nor by power, but by My Spirit, says the Lord of hosts."* (Zech. 4:6). Spoiler alert: The power is not in us being winsome or clever of speech. The power is in the Word of God. Unleash it. Let it out to do its work. And then stand back and watch the Spirit have His way.

What are some qualities of one who is teachable? He learns from others, from experience, from nature. He studies to know the truth found in Scripture. He is open to change. He is discerning. He is humble. One common denominator I've noticed in people who are not teachable is a lack of humility. All learning starts when we admit we **don't** know everything and can learn from everybody we meet.

Humility says, "Everything I have (talents, skills, looks, intelligence, etc.) was given to me (1 Cor. 4:7), I didn't create myself, nor add to the package." Humility also considers all men to be my equal and doesn't look down on anybody. Why should we keep learning? Paul tells Timothy, *"Be diligent to present yourself approved to God as a workman who does not need to be ashamed, accurately handling the word of truth."* (2 Tim. 2:15). Paul goes on, *"All Scripture is inspired by God and profitable for teaching, for reproof, for correction, for training in righteousness so that the man of God may be adequate, equipped for every good work."* (2 Tim. 3:16,17). Apparently, God expects us to know and teach the truth of His word. If we stick to Scripture without throwing in our two cents, we needn't be ashamed because we are accurate in our teaching. Beware of the preacher who only preaches topically. Is he an ear-tickler?

So how do we do this? We feast on the meat of the Word of God. We snack on the promises of God. We exercise the worship and praise of God. Did not King David leap and dance before the Lord? (2 Sam. 6:16). As with any exercise program, we must be committed to see it through. Our growth doesn't happen overnight, it's a lifelong pursuit. The Bible says, *"Do not be conformed to this world, but be transformed by the renewing of your mind..."* (Rom. 12:2)

March 2, 2021

Know God or No God

Sixty-six times In Ezekiel, in one form or another, God says, *"that they will know that I am the Lord."* In my opinion, the key verse for this prophetic book is Ezekiel 26:22,23: *"It is not for your sake, O house of Israel, that I am about to act, but for My holy name...I will vindicate the holiness of My great name."*

Why is God so concerned about His name? Why is one of the "big 10," *"You shall not take the name of the Lord your God in vain"* with a specific warning, *"for the Lord will not leave him unpunished who takes His name in vain."* (Exo. 20:7)? I cringe when I hear people use God's or Jesus' name as a swear word. Two things come to mind. First, they don't know the God whom they're defiling, and second, they don't have a very broad vocabulary.

When a nation rejects God and so easily and often profanes His holy name—LOOK OUT. If America isn't already there, we're so close you could throw a rock and hit it. Review some of the signs foretold by Paul to Timothy, *"...**in the last days**...men will be lovers of self, lovers of money, boastful, arrogant, revilers...unholy...without self-control...haters of good...lovers of pleasure rather than lovers of God...avoid such men as these."* (2 Tim 3:1-5).

In our opening verse from Ezekiel, God announces, through His prophet, that He is about to act to destroy Israel and surrounding nations. What is He planning? You can read the litany of judgments from chapter 6 through chapter 39 of Ezekiel. Not a pretty picture for the nations. But I tell you that to tell you this. God's protection of His name hasn't lessened in the two and a half millennia since Ezekiel spoke. His vindication of His "great name" WILL be accomplished. That's the beauty of studying fulfilled prophecy. It validates God's warnings, which He always gives before He carries out judgment. And everything He says will happen, will happen. We have no excuse because of all the warnings in the Bible.

America, along with the whole world, is rushing toward God's judgment. Not just for profaning His name, but for rejecting His love, mercy, and forgiveness through Jesus Christ's death to pay for OUR sins. Think about this. You have a legitimate debt that you could never repay and you're in a 3rd-world prison for life because of it. A distant uncle hears of your problem and ponies up and covers your debt. Rather than *thank* him and do whatever you can *for* him to prove your thankfulness, you mock and think, "what a sucker." And he only spent money on you. What if he had a son, your cousin, and somehow, he killed your cousin, and that act paid your debt. Would you feel the same way toward him? Do you think your ingratitude could offend your uncle? Replace uncle with God. Replace cousin with Jesus. Replace 3rd-world prison with hell. That's the future for rejecters of Christ's death on their behalf.

Why do I care? I've already got my ticket punched and I'm ready when God calls. It's simple, really. Once I was in that 3rd-world prison and now know the difference between a life without Jesus and a life with Him. I had a lot of pride and self-sufficiency. Still have more than I like, but sanctification is a life-long process, and I am on the right path. The ruler of this world has blinded the eyes of the rejecters to the point of refusing to see their need for someone to pay their debt. Brothers, the debt has been paid. All you have to do is say no to the world and yes to Jesus. It really is that easy. That's why so many miss it. They think God couldn't possibly love me after the things I've done. Trust me. God knows your darkest secrets…and loves you anyway. Don't let the devil's lies keep you from an eternity in heaven that is without pain, sorrow, death, and utter darkness. The Bible says in hell, "*there will be weeping and gnashing of teeth*" (Matt. 25:30), a place filled with pain and darkness that never ends.

Your ultimate future is an either/or scenario. Either you will **know God** or there will be **no God**. Before you say "great, I don't want Him anyway," reread the previous paragraph and make a conscious decision. You'll live with it for eternity. If you want to see your spiritual condition from God's perspective, visit the *Steps to Salvation* Appendix at the back of the book.

Thanks for taking the time to read. If you have questions, drop an email. We'll get back to you.

March 4, 2021

America in the Crosshairs

*"...the Lord has a case against the inhabitants of the land **because there is no faithfulness or kindness or knowledge of God in the land.** There is swearing, deception, murder, stealing and adultery. They employ violence, so that bloodshed follows bloodshed. Therefore the land mourns, and everyone who lives in it languishes...My people are destroyed for lack of knowledge."* (Hosea 4:1-3,6)

This was written over 2,700 years ago and if it isn't a wakeup call for the church in America today, then I don't know what it will take to shake us from our lethargy. God's patience is without equal. But it has an expiration date.

In the 4th chapter of 1 Peter, God clearly spells out His plan just as He did for Israel (see *"Nothing to See Here"* and *"Know God or No God"*). *"**The end of all things is near;** therefore be of sound judgment and sober spirit for the purpose of prayer."* (v.7) *"Beloved, do not be surprised at the fiery ordeal among you, which comes upon you for your testing, as though some strange thing were happening to you."* (v.12) *"For **it is time for judgment to begin with the household of God**; and if it begins with us first, what will be the outcome for those who do not obey the gospel of God?"* (v. 17)

It's that last statement I want to focus on. Judgment. Just the word instills angst, even fear. But for believers in Jesus Christ, it should be a cause of rejoicing. All of the "swearing, deception, murder, stealing, and adultery" that we thought "they" were getting away with is on the docket. And it will "begin with the household of God." What does that mean?

Proverbs 6:16 begins a list of six things the Lord hates: pride, lies, bloodshed of the innocent, hearts that plan wickedness, evil acts, and troublemakers (in churches). Not everybody who sits in a pew is a Christian. The Bible says, *"You will know them by their fruits"* (Matt. 7:16). If the thought of judgment worries you, there are a couple possible reasons. First, you know you're guilty and punishment awaits. Or, second, you have confessed your sin and turned to Jesus for salvation, but your faith that Jesus took ALL your sins is weak and the devil continues his bombardment of lies trying to keep you on the sideline.

Consider your "fruit." If you are a child of the King and walking in the light, what Paul says applies to you, *"for the fruit of the Light consists in all goodness and righteousness and truth"* (Eph. 5:9). Don't let Satan steal your victory, your hope, your confidence. Christians aren't perfect; we still sin. But we ARE forgiven, cleansed, and accepted by God as unblemished.

If you're not producing the right kind of fruit, but find yourself on the list of six, perhaps you've bought the lie that going to church and reciting liturgy and rote prayers gets your ticket punched. I've got great news for you. It's not too late...yet. In humility, recognize that your sin hasn't been paid for and you are separated from a holy God, that there's nothing YOU can do to avoid the sentence of guilty. Believe that Jesus paid your debt by His death and resurrection.

God's judgment IS real. And it's coming to a church near you. While you still breathe, you are still in the race. The warning sirens are blaring. The enemy is ramping up his attacks, multiplying his lies, and grinning in glee every time he keeps a sinner from believing the truth. Don't be like the ones Jesus talked about, *"Not everyone who says to me, 'Lord, Lord,' will enter the kingdom of heaven, but he who does the will of My Father who is in heaven will enter. Many will say to Me on that day, 'Lord, Lord, did we not prophesy in Your name, and in Your name cast out demons, and in Your name perform many miracles?' And I will declare to them, 'I never knew you; depart from me, you who practice lawlessness.'"* (Matt. 7:21-23)

God is watching America, waiting for those who will, to repent and come to Him. The previous verses make it clear not all who attend church will be included. Don't be one of those who thinks you've been good enough, given enough to charity, or never murdered or committed adultery, and that's your basis for hope. Jesus was very clear, *"I am **the** way and **the** truth and **the** life, **no one** comes to the Father but **through Me**."* (John 14:6). If you want to know how to avoid God's judgment see *Steps to Salvation* in the back of this book.

March 6, 2021

If Jesus Were Only a Man

Important events in human history are always accompanied by fanfare, parades, crowds, and endless media coverage. Except once. And for a seemingly insignificant event some 2,000 years ago, it is by far the MOST IMPORTANT event in all of human history—past, present, and future even without the hoopla. I'm referring, of course, to the resurrection of Jesus Christ on the third day after His death.

Counting the disciples and the people Jesus appeared to, there were probably fewer than 600 who saw Him alive after He was risen. Not exactly your ticker-tape parade. Nevertheless, this one event will have an impact for all eternity on every person who has ever lived. If that's true, why don't we hear more about Him? Why are there so many religions?

The answer is simple, but not widely accepted because the ruler of this world—Satan, the father of lies—has been wildly successful in his disinformation campaign. The lies we see in today's media are not new, nor invented by politicians. It began in the Garden of Eden when the devil asked Eve, *"Indeed, has God said..."* (Gen. 3:1). (As an aside and topic for another discussion, Eve is a perfect example of bad decisions made by not knowing God's word.)

The gullibility of many people to swallow Satan's lies shouldn't surprise us. The Bible tells us, *"the foolishness of God is wiser than men"* (1 Cor. 1:25). The Bible also says, in Romans 1, *"**wrath of God**...**against**...**men who suppress the truth** in unrighteousness"* (v.18), *"that which is known about **God is evident** within them; for God made it evident to them"* (v.19), *"they are **without excuse.**"* (v.20) *"...they became **futile** in their speculations, and their **foolish** heart was darkened"* (v.21). Fools. That's what God calls men who reject Him and His truth. The rest of Romans 1 is a devastating description of the downward spiral into total depravity of those who "profess to be wise" (v.22). Consider this phrase, "God gave them over." Three times. First to **impurity** (v.24), second to **degrading passions** (v.26), finally to a **depraved mind** (v.28). That sound like anybody you know?

If Jesus were only a man, none of what I've said would be true and I would be numbered among the fools. But He wasn't, and it is, and I'm not. He IS God. He DID rise from the dead. He is THE ONLY WAY to the Father.

Why so many religions? Again the source is a lie. Jesus said clearly, *"I am **the** way and **the** truth and **the** life, no one comes to the Father but through Me"* (John 14:6). But believing that requires humility and submission. Man loves his pride. It often takes a crisis, where we are really down and out before we realize we can't meet God's standard of righteousness. Frankly, we don't really want to. Sin is fun. Sin feels good…for a time. But sin separates us from God. Sin enslaves us to follow our lusts. It's a slippery slope that we don't realize we're even on, sometimes until it's too late.

With the exception of Biblical Christianity, all other religions have at their core, a works-based salvation. Again the Bible is not vague: *"For by grace you have been saved through faith, and that not of yourselves it is a **gift of God, not as a result of works** so that no one may boast"* (Eph. 2:8,9). Let's be clear. There is NO amount of good works you can do to restore your relationship to a holy God. The Bible says, "all *our righteous deeds are like a filthy garment*" (Isa. 64:6). You wouldn't dare try to visit the King in those clothes. Fortunately, in Christ, we are clothed with a robe of righteousness (Isa. 61:10).

You may be saying, "so what?" Or you may be saying, "Sounds interesting. What do I need to do?" To the first, I encourage you to take stock of what gods you are serving and ask yourself, "What is the ultimate destination of this path?" To the curious, I invite you to visit our *Steps to Salvation* Appendix for a detailed look at God's perspective of sin and how to get connected with Him. If you have questions, you can contact us and we will answer them or point you to someone who can.

Thanks for stopping by.

March 8, 2021

Majoring on Minors

"*Surely the Lord God does nothing **unless** He reveals His secret counsel to His servants the prophets*" (Amos 3:7). How much warning is enough? One hundred years? Two thousand years? It took Noah over 100 years to build the ark, during which time he practiced righteousness. Then the rain came. It's been over two millennia since Jesus Christ walked the earth and warned us that the end is near. And yet we go on like everything will always be like it always was. That's what the people of Noah's day thought too. Then the rain came.

What will our "rain" look like? What will God use this time? He promised never to flood the earth again. So we know it won't be the same method of destruction. But speculating about *what* it will be rather than *why* it will be is majoring in the minors. The "why" should be our focus. God's countdown clock has begun. It actually began in the Garden of Eden some 6,000 or so years ago when God told Satan, "*He shall bruise you on the head, and you shall bruise Him on the heel*" (Gen. 3:15). This is a reference to the crucifixion of Jesus in which, though He was wounded (the Bible says, "…for our transgressions" [Isa. 53:5]), totally defeated sin and death.

Six millennia is a long time to wait for the fulfillment of a promise. But the Bible says, "*The Lord is not slow about His promise, as some count slowness, but is **patient toward you**, not wishing for any to perish but for all to come to repentance*" (2 Pet. 3:9). Personalize it. It says, "patient toward you." Do you know God's patience today?

Knowing that a) God cannot lie (Titus 1:2), b) the Bible is true cover to cover (2Tim. 3:16), c) Every prophecy either has been or will be fulfilled to the letter in God's time, and d) death ushers us into eternity (Heb. 9:27), the "why" is critical to understand.

We've already seen that God is patient. He's also not capricious. He doesn't wake up some morning and say, "Let's see how much Bob can handle today." But He *IS* holy and cannot tolerate sin. Our sin separated us from Him. If it's not dealt with according to His plan, we're separated from Him for all eternity. That is the "why" of His planned destruction. We're guilty and no excuse will sway the heavenly Judge. The penalty must be paid. Fortunately for us, it has been paid, once for all by Jesus' death on the cross.

The world order is changing. Fear is the weapon of choice to control the sheep. Antichrist is not going to suddenly appear from nowhere and create a one-world government, a one-world currency, a financial system in which you must have "a mark" to buy or sell (Rev. 13:17) and demand your worship. No, it will be gradual like boiling a frog by slowly turning up the fire. Sound far-fetched? It's already started. Easing mask requirements ONLY for those who have their vaccinations. You'll get an ID card of some kind verifying your shots. And, since ID cards can be stolen or forged, you'll probably have a chip inserted like you do for your dog. I'm just sayin'.

How close are we on God's doomsday clock? I don't know. Neither does anybody else. It may be 11:59 or it may not. But why take any chances on an event that will take the whole world by surprise. Think back to all the hoopla over Y2K at the turn of the century. All computer-based electronics were supposed to crash because of a 2-digit year instead of a 4-digit year in their programming. Do you remember anything crashing? Fear. It caused many companies to spend millions and millions of dollars they didn't need to because somebody said "boo."

God's warnings are more serious because He doesn't play games with our eternity. It should be an easy choice because there are only two destinations from which to choose. Unfortunately, they're both labeled Heaven. But one is a lie. Do you think anybody in their right mind would choose hell if it were labeled correctly? Surprise. Many do. They refuse to bend the knee to God's sovereignty because of pride. You know, I don't need no stinkin' directions.

The clock is ticking. God has given ample warning that judgment is coming. Don't be left at the door after it's been shut like the five foolish virgins (Matt. 7:2,3,12). The only thing you'll hear from Jesus Himself is, "*I do not know you.*" Be like the five prudent virgins (showing thought for the future) who brought extra oil for their lamps and went in with the bridegroom (Jesus). Jesus followed up this parable by saying, "*Be on the alert then, for you do not know the day nor the hour.*" Tick, tick, tick…Our "*Steps to Salvation*" Appendix will help you understand what time it is…for you.

March 10, 2021

The Age of Reason...Is Dead

"'Come now and let us reason together' says the Lord, 'though your sins are as scarlet they will be as white as snow'" (Isa.1:18). Pride and prejudice are more than a book title by Jane Austen. They are roadblocks to living in harmony with our neighbors. Society has become so polarized by political affiliation and indoctrination that common sense and reason have left the building. Could that be the reason we only see near-party-line votes in Congress?

King Solomon said, *"The king's heart is like channels of water in the hand of the Lord; He turns it wherever He wishes"* (Prov. 21:1). Throughout history, God has used those in positions of authority to carry out His purposes. Biblical examples abound where we also get the "back story," God's reasoning behind His actions (e.g. Pharoah, Nebuchadnezzar, Herod, etc.). Though we can't see it, God uses despots as well as godly leaders as means to His ends.

No matter how crazy our current politics seem, nothing sneaks up on God or thwarts His plans. In fact it seems that the crazier and un-reasoned something is, you can be sure God is using the so-called "wisdom" of man to bring about His desired outcome. I won't turn this into a political rant, though there are certainly enough examples to make it an easy exercise. But the focus is on our staying the course regardless of society's sinfulness. Remember, we're on the winning team. I've read the end of His-story.

Could this also be the reason many reject God's FREE offer of a restored relationship with Him? They've been blinded by Satan, the ruler of this world, and his wisdom; it is demonic, evil, filled with lies. When we think highly of ourselves, we've bought his lies hook, line, etc. We're just waiting to be reeled in by the captain of the losing team.

Think about this. Can you name one society anywhere or anytime on earth that went from a state of debauchery where lying was normal, aberrant sex was normal, and disregard for other people's person or property was normal, that ever went back to a "civilized" existence? Me neither. So what's my point? Only that every time in Biblical his-tory when things got to this stage, God's judgment wasn't far behind. One time that stands out when it was delayed was when Nineveh, estimated at about 600,000 people, repented because of Jonah's preaching about coming judgment. But it only lasted about 100 years and they were back where they started, maybe worse. And then judgment came.

It doesn't take a rocket scientist to assess the data that bombards us daily, see the deteriorating condition of the country and world we live in, and conclude something is VERY wrong. But therein is the problem. A brilliant mind isn't required, but honesty, truth, and standards definitely are. Unfortunately, none of these seems in abundant supply. When God created the earth and everything in it, He created "them" male and female (Gen. 1:27). It is so obvious that we even refer to inanimate objects that fit together as being the male connector or the female connector.

It's ironic that all the video games played are written in languages that depend solely on logic and reason. If the player does this, then that happens. But these are foreign concepts to many who play. One of the first statements in a last will and testament goes something like this, "being of sound mind..." But isn't that what many estate squabbles between heirs are about? Grandpa can't leave it to his dog, that's nuts.

The root of all problems in society, whether racism, crime against persons and property, greed, or you name it, can be traced back to rejection of God and His standards. The Bible has the answer for all man's problems, but apart from a spiritual revival, nothing will change. It will only get worse. This is a wakeup call to all who name Christ as their Savior. Our enemy is not the Democrat or Republican party. It's not Mitch McConnell or Chuck Schumer. Our enemy is not even flesh and blood (Eph. 6:12). So our weapons are not guns and swords or tanks and missiles. Our weapons are the Word of God and prayer. Those who display the philosophies, attitudes, and political differences we despise need our prayer for their salvation. This world is as good as it will be for them. Their eternity is bleak at best. We can't say we love God whom we have not seen if we hate our neighbor whom we have seen (1 John 4:20). Think about it.

Our "*Steps to Salvation*" Appendix will help you guide someone through God's invitation to reason with Him.

March 22, 2021

How Wide is the Narrow Way?

Scripture tells us there are two ways with two gates, the wide way which many are on and the narrow way which few are on. (Matt. 7:13,14) Are there few *because* the way is narrow and more won't fit? No. It's narrow because to walk it, one must come empty-handed, and few are willing to give up everything. There are crowds on the wide way because they haven't had to give up anything to be on it. Is that important? Don't they both lead to the same place? One would think so by the false labeling on the wide way. The narrow way is labeled "Heaven—only believers in Jesus Christ allowed." The wide way is labeled heaven too, but there are no restrictions, i.e. all types of religious folks are welcome.

There's only one problem—and it's a BIG one. The wide way DOESN'T lead to heaven. Ask yourself, "How can I trust a map made by the 'father of lies,' Satan? (John 8:44). Do you think anyone would be on the wide way if they knew the truth that it leads to hell (destruction)? (Matt. 7:13). Sadly, the answer is 'yes they would' and yes, they are. How is that possible?

We live in a visible world. There's also an invisible world filled with an entire spirit population. Some are angels under orders from God to be messengers to and protect His church. Then there's the demonic side who are under the devil's control and play havoc with the world. Fortunately for believers, God has limited the devil's ability to tempt and mess with us (1 Cor. 10:13), though he tries his hardest. The Bible says, *"The thief* [Satan] *comes only to steal and kill and destroy."* (John 10:10). So don't be surprised when fiery trials blindside you. The demons have their marching orders. If you haven't read it, *The Screwtape Letters* by C.S. Lewis is must-read.

There are many reasons people reject the gospel message that God loves me, my sin separated me from Him, Jesus paid the debt my sin created with His death on the cross and resurrection from the grave. Primarily, the rejection is rooted in pride and selfishness. We don't want accountability to a God whose standard is righteousness. We want what we want, and it becomes a (little g) god to us. We've all heard stories—maybe even been taken in by one—of con men who are smooth talkers and can make lies sound like truth. Satan has had millennia to perfect his craft. We succumb because the promise of easy wealth or increased popularity or (fill in the blank) appeals to our greed and self-centeredness.

So, what do we really have to give up that "they" get to keep? Here's the first ten from a long alphabetical list: anger, bitterness, clamor, deceit, envy, friendship with the world, greed, hypocrisy, idols, jealousy, and many, many more. Doesn't really sound so bad, does it? What would the world be like if everybody rid themselves of these "character" qualities? The world would be like heaven where the Bible says in heaven there will be no tears, no death, no mourning, no crying, no pain (Rev. 4:21). But because man holds firmly to these qualities, earth can never become heaven. That alone should be motivation to find and stay on the narrow way…but it isn't. Man laughs and mocks God's plan for redemption. "I don't need no stinkin' redemption," he says. But God will have the final laugh (Ps. 2).

To answer our opening question about the width of the narrow way, it's wide enough. Wide enough for anyone who wants to humble themselves and come according to God's terms. Jesus said, "*I am the way and the truth and the life. No one comes to the Father but through Me*" (John 14:6). Jesus said, "*…the one who comes to Me I will certainly not cast out*" (John 6:37). Sounds pretty all-inclusive to me.

If you want to know more about God's plan for YOUR salvation, visit our "*Steps to Salvation*" Appendix. Thanks for reading.

March 25, 2021

You in the Word—the Word in you

We hear a lot about truth today. There's your truth, my truth, "truth" about global warming, Dr. Fauci's truth, which seems dependent on which way the wind blows. How can there be so many different truths? The answer is easy. They're *not* all true. Period. Spoiler alert: people lie.

But there is *one truth* that is immutable, never changes, never been proven wrong, and on which we can base our daily lives as well as our eternity. Wow. You'd think people would rush to embrace that kind of truth. You'd think. But they don't. Why? Lots of reasons. The truth conflicts with our agenda. The truth requires change, sometimes drastic. The truth reveals our selfishness. The truth demands accountability. The truth exposes our corrupt nature. And there are many more.

It's hard to understand, when so many seek answers, so many are discouraged by society's shallow solutions, and government runs amok, why more folks don't turn to the *one source* of truth: God's Word. That's an easy one too. Those who don't know Jesus can't understand it because they are "natural" men (1 Cor. 2:14).

But what about those who claim to be followers of Jesus Christ? Many believe they have gotten their "ticket to heaven" punched but they keep one foot in the world. The shiny things are just too appealing, and they haven't **taken up their cross daily** to become a true disciple of His (Luke 9:23). It's sad to know that Jesus' unfathomable love isn't enough to rivet our focus on Him as an act of gratitude. We assume. We expect. We take for granted. There's a risk here for those in this category.

Jesus said, *"If you love me you will keep my commandments"* (John 14:15). Most of us wouldn't consider ourselves idol worshippers. But when shiny objects usurp our focus, our time and energy, they have become to us, gods. And what does the first commandment say, *"You shall have **no other gods** before Me"* (Exo. 20:3). There's a reason this is first. If we don't get this one right, the other nine don't really matter. We're already toast.

Are you having trouble in your family? Maybe this is the reason. Listen to what God says, *"I am a jealous God, visiting the iniquity of the fathers on the children, on the third and the fourth generations of those who hate Me…"* (Exo. 20:5). Hate is a strong word. But it shows us God's heart and how He views those of us who haven't put Him first.

Maybe some self-evaluation is in order. Where are you on your spiritual journey? Everybody's on one whether we think so or not. We *are* spiritual beings who will live forever. Think about this. Do we clam up when the discussion turns from the weather, sports, or politics to things of God? Try this the next time you're in a family discussion. After allowing, say, a political rant for some time, ask, "What does God say about that?". If you hear crickets, you know you've hit a sore spot.

For those of us who name Christ as Savior and friend, everybody is watching to see if we really believe and live what we say. The hypocrisy that is so rampant in politics today also dwells in you and me. Do we recognize it? Be sure that others do. What's the solution? First, in humility, we need to ask forgiveness from God and our family for not modeling the ways of God on a more consistent basis. Next, commit to eliminating anything that has replaced God as *numero uno* in our lives. Then develop the habit of allowing God's word to penetrate and permeate our minds and hearts on a daily basis. Allow and expect the Holy Spirit to change you. He will.

If, as part of your self-evaluation, you're not sure where you stand with God, maybe a refresher down the path to salvation would be in order. You can find it in our *"Steps to Salvation"* Appendix in the back of this book. If you *are* sure, praise God. What is your plan to get and keep both feet out of the world? Remember, Jesus said, "daily." Thanks for stopping by.

April 6, 2021

Sunday Was Easter

I am still basking in the glow of the Resurrection celebration. We had two dozen people at my house, eight of them college students who came home from college with my granddaughter. We ate, played outdoor games, had good discussions about living the Christian life. Yesterday, I left the house at 3:15 AM to take them to the Denver airport. When I got home, I began reading 1 Peter. I couldn't get past the first five verses without stopping to give thanks. I want to share some of that with you.

Let your mind dwell on these words for a few minutes: great mercy, living hope, resurrection of Jesus Christ from the dead, imperishable, undefiled, will not fade, reserved in heaven for you. The source? God's great mercy. The substance? Living hope. The vehicle? The resurrection of Jesus Christ from the dead. The timing? Doesn't matter, we've got a reservation.

If we ever needed *any* hope, let alone *living* hope, it's now, in the shadow of the worst political climate I've seen in my lifetime. The church is under attack. Christians are being discriminated against by power-hungry politicians allowing themselves to be influenced and controlled by the evil puppet master, Satan. The Bible is so clear as to the consequences of a nation turning from God. You see it time and time again with reference to Israel, both *to* them and to *their enemies.*

God is a God of patience, but it has an expiration date. In my last post, I asked where you are on your spiritual journey. I think a broader discussion is called for. The Bible tells us we are spiritual people (1 Thess. 5:23; James 2:26, Rom. 8:10). As such, our spirits will live forever. 1 John 2:17 says, *"The world is passing away, and also its lusts; but the one who does the will of God lives forever."* We know our bodies can't live forever, so there must be a part of us that does. We're told in Galatians 6:8, *"For the one who sows to his own flesh will from the flesh reap corruption, but the one who sows to the Spirit will from the Spirit reap eternal life."*

Many are on their spiritual journey and don't realize there are only two destinations, heaven or hell. Think again about the words in paragraph two. Then think about these words: mourning, crying, pain, death…forever. Do I even need to ask which environment you would rather be in? That's the message of Easter—of the Resurrection—LIFE. And joy, and peace, and unity, and…and…and…in the presence of Jesus.

Here's the truth. If you're not interested in Jesus or the things of God now, then continue to shun them and you won't be bothered by Him ever, throughout eternity. Additionally, if you aren't interested in the *people of God* on earth, then your companions in hell will be the *"cowardly, the unbelieving, the abominable, the murderers, immoral persons, sorcerers, idolaters, and all liars, whose part is in the lake that burns with fire and brimstone"* (Rev. 21:8). Are these your circle of friends now? Do you want them to be for eternity? While you breathe, God is calling you, offering you a living hope through His Son, Jesus. Personalize the message of Easter, that Jesus rose from the dead FOR YOU. As our current president would say, "c'mon, man."

Heaven will be amazingly amazing (hard to put it into words grand enough). YOU can be there. God promised that *"…whoever believes in Him* [Jesus] *will not perish* [in hell] *but have everlasting LIFE"* (John 3:16). C'mon, man. Make the right decision. If you need more detail about what God thinks about you and how you can be restored to a Father-son relationship with Him, check out our *"Steps To Salvation"* Appendix in the back of this book. Thanks for your time. Hope to see you there.

April 10, 2021

My Dad Is...

"and the glory of sons is their fathers." (Prov. 17:6). I remember growing up sometimes included brag sessions of guys' dads. Some were rich. Some had cool jobs. Some, frankly, were bums. Mine was somewhere in the middle. I never lacked a roof, a meal, or clothes. There was even money for piano lessons...until I decided at about 10 years old, I would rather play baseball, which it turned out I wasn't very good at. Shoulda stayed with the keyboard.

My dad passed away about 25 years ago, my mom a few years later. But I'm not an orphan because my Heavenly Father told me, *"Be strong and courageous, do not be afraid or tremble at them, for the Lord God is the One who goes with you. He will not fail you or forsake you"* (Deut. 31:6). This morning, my mind started wandering and I came across this thought, "Am I proud of my (heavenly) Father? Do I brag about Him to others?" The beat-around-the-bush answer is, "mostly." And I asked myself, "Why not all the time?" I didn't like the answer. Too often I'm self-centered not *"regarding others as more important than* [my] *yourselves"* (Phil. 2:3).

When I think about all that my heavenly Father has done for me—and the list is long—I can't help but thank and praise Him. So it seems that if that's the result of remembering the list, and I want to change "mostly" to "all the time," I need to train my mind to *"dwell on these things**...and the God of peace will be with you"* (Phil. 4:8,9). ** *Whatever is true, honorable, right, pure, lovely, good repute, excellence, worthy of praise...*

How's your relationship with the Father of lights? (Jas. 1:17) Are you proud of Him? Do you boast of what He has done in your life? I believe our time is short before God calls us home. How short? I don't know. It could be today, tomorrow or a hundred years from now.

The point is that there are many who don't have this relationship with our Father, and you may be the only Bible they read. Is your verbal message about Jesus strong and backed up by your lifestyle message? Or do you waver a bit when the going gets rough? Reread the verse from Deuteronomy above, He WILL NOT FAIL YOU OR FORSAKE YOU.

If you're not totally in the game, there's still time. Get off the bench and tell someone about Jesus...TODAY. If all this sounds foreign to you and you don't have a relationship with the God of Creation, the God who sustains the universe with His Word, check out our "*Steps to Salvation*" Appendix in the back of this book. .

April 12, 2021

Choose Your Garden

The Bible mentions several gardens. There's the Garden of Eden, created perfect, filled with good things albeit not without temptations. Even though man sinned and was booted out and the garden remains unoccupied, the world still compares a place with ideal conditions to the Garden of Eden. I've been to some of those places, e.g. Hawaii, the Caribbean to name two. Then there's the Garden of Gethsemane where we see deception, treachery, betrayal, failed trials (*"Could you not keep watch for one hour?"* Mark 14:37), but also God's master plan at work. This was the beginning of the end for Christ on earth.

In another writing in this book entitled *"How Does Your Garden Grow"*. We looked at your garden of redeemed souls whom you have led to Christ. We recognized that God does not hold us accountable for the success of our witnessing, just our faithfulness. He is the true gardener; we're just planters and waterers. Today, I'd like to look at gardens as places of opportunity.

If given a choice, I'm pretty sure most of us would choose Eden over Gethsemane. But would that be the best choice? Ask yourself, "What does our Eden really offer?" To be sure, beautiful things, comfort, possibly a life of ease. And someday when we reach heaven, we'll have all that and much more. But in this world, isn't there a risk of complacency, of becoming lukewarm when our faith is not challenged, our passion for the lost is not stirred, and our vision of "the great commission" dims?

If God didn't intend for us to be involved in the soul-harvest once we believed in Jesus, He'd take us home. Then who would plant and water? Yesterday I read in Proverbs, *"He who is wise wins souls."* (Prov. 11:30). Don't we all want to be considered wise? There's the answer: win souls.

When we choose Gethsemane over Eden, we can expect the same things Jesus met with, even from his closest companions. We *should expect* that because Jesus said, *"In the world you have tribulation, but take courage, I have overcome the world."* (John 16:33). That's not an empty pep talk from the coach. We have been given the full armor of God to wear into the battle: truth, righteousness, gospel of peace, shield of faith, helmet of salvation, and the sword of the Spirit (Eph. 6:13-17). If we're comfortable in our "Eden," complacent in our life of ease, then getting dressed for battle probably isn't high on our priority list.

I was a Drill Sergeant in the Army during Vietnam. When a trainee didn't jump to obey an order, there was always some form of discipline. Brothers and sisters, we are in God's army and He has given us orders (*"Go into all the world..."*). Is He less worthy of our undivided obedience than a lowly Army Sergeant? *"...do not be surprised at the fiery ordeal among you, which comes upon you for your testing,"* (Pet. 4:12). And don't be surprised if some of it isn't for discipline purposes.

In our Gethsemane, we will have trials. But rejoice. We're not going alone and without weapons (*"Our weapons are divinely powerful for the destruction of fortresses."* 2 Cor. 10:4). So man up. Get dressed for battle. And move out.

There is much encouragement and hope presented in this book. If you're new in your walk with Jesus, make sure you're attending and involved in a Bible-believing church and reading your Bible every day. If this is all new to you and you'd like to know more, visit our *"Steps to Salvation"* Appendix in the back of this book. Hope to see you on the battlefield.

April 16, 2021

Looking for Work

A few good men. It seems everybody is looking for a few good men. The Marine Corps, any employer who has openings, any group of would-be brides, the God of heaven. I'm sure, if you know Jesus Christ as your Lord and Savior, you've asked yourself, "What is God's will for me?" Today, I'm going to answer that question.

We're all probably familiar with 2 Cor. 5:17, "*If anyone is in Christ, he is a new creature...*" But I wonder how many of us know the next verse: "*Now all these things are from God, who **reconciled** us to Himself through Christ and gave us the **ministry of reconciliation**...*" And there it is, God's will. Are you looking for a place to plug in at your church? How about starting or joining the Ministry of Reconciliation? What is that and why do we need it? A simple definition of reconciliation is this: reuniting, bringing back together again. For our purposes, it means showing others the way (back) to God.

How does that apply to me? I have no seminary or Bible school training. Do you know Jesus? Do you have a Bible? You're qualified. In its simplest form, it means sharing the good news that Jesus came to earth to reconcile sinners to His Father. Your role is just to tell people the story. God doesn't keep score of how many you talk to that turn from a life of sin. The results are the Holy Spirit's job.

As to why we need it, it's because sin has separated us from a holy God. We sin. Therefore, we're under judgment. Romans 3:23 says, "*For all have sinned and fall short of the glory of God.*" Three chapters later we learn the penalty for sin, "*For the wages of sin is death,*" but thank God it doesn't stop there, "*but the **free gift** of God is eternal life in Christ Jesus our Lord.*" (Rom. 6:23).

Have you ever tried to sell something? You know how many objections, real or not, people can come up with. Too expensive, bad timing, I don't need it. And hundreds more. In a way we're sharing the gospel, hoping they will bite. But price can't be an objection because it's totally free...to us, but it cost Jesus His life to offer mankind reconciliation.

I don't fish, but I know if I wanted to catch fish, I'd have to go where they are. Sharing the good news is like that. Fortunately, you don't need a large pond with thousands of fish. You only need one person who needs a Savior. And they're all around us; in our churches, our families, in our neighborhood, at our jobs, we just have to *"preach the word; be ready in season and out of season, reprove, rebuke, exhort, with great patience and instruction."* (2 Tim. 4:2).

If you've never shared your faith because you don't feel like you know enough, you've bought into the enemy's lie. You have your own story to tell about who you were before you met Jesus, how He changed you, and who you are now (a new creature). There are many good ways to start a conversation about God. My two favorites are *The Way of The Master* and *Evangelism Explosion*. Both start with simple questions. "Have you ever considered what happens after you die?" "If you were to die and stand before God and He asked you, 'Why should I let you into heaven?' what would you say?"

I firmly believe that all Christians, myself included, are educated way beyond our obedience. I don't mean college degrees or that kind of education. I mean, if we've read any of the Bible, we've come across one or more commands that we're not obeying. I don't say that to condemn anyone but to encourage us to test our faith and see how faithful God is to *"strongly support those whose heart is completely His."* (2 Chron. 16:9). As I said earlier, God doesn't hold us accountable for results. That's totally in His hands. But He does demand obedience.

After reading today's message, you have at least one answer to the question, "What is God's will for me?" Now it's up to you to obey or not. Choose wisely and get to work.

April 19, 2021

Biblical Illiteracy—a Self-Inflicted Wound *

"I can't memorize Scripture; nothing seems to stick." "I don't have the time and I don't understand a lot of it." I'm sure you've heard these excuses and more in discussions with those who give them, thus exposing their lack of understanding of the importance of treasuring God's Word in our hearts, *"that we may not sin against Him"* (Ps. 119:11). It's precisely this lack of priority, lack of faith in God's timeless Word, that makes many in the church "low-hanging fruit"* for the wiles of the devil. And then we wonder why God doesn't answer our prayers. The Bible says, *"If you abide in Me and **My words abide in you,** ask whatever you wish and it will be done for you"* (John 15:7). So what part of "My words abide in you" isn't clear?

That's what I love about God's Word. We don't need advanced degrees to understand the message. Most of God's promises have a condition attached: if you, then I…fill in the blank. We're just not willing to do the "if you(s)." Why not? I believe it's because we don't really know the God who made the promise. And in not knowing, we don't love Him or trust Him. Isn't that sad? He's given us everything in Christ, promised us everything in Christ, prepared a place for us in heaven with Christ. The irony is that the exact thing we shun—God's Word—is the exact thing that brings us closer to Him: *"Establish Your Word to Your servant as that which produces reverence for You"* (Ps. 119:38). A great passage on God's mercy and faithfulness is Nehemiah 9, especially verses 16-31.

In the list of God's armor that we are to take up for the battle against the *"spiritual forces of wickedness* (Eph. 6:12)," there is only one offensive weapon: the *"sword of the Spirit which is the Word of God* (Eph. 6:17)." If you've served in the military, especially if you've seen combat, you know that if you only have one offensive weapon, you guard it with your life, you make sure it's in top working order at all times because your life depends on it. Spiritual warfare is no different—just the weapons. Our "sword" can only remain sharp with constant use. It's been said that if a man's Bible is falling apart (from use), then it's very likely he isn't.

Think about that. What battle are you in? What weapon(s) are you using? Even when Jesus was tempted by the devil in the wilderness after 40 days of fasting which would have left him hungry and weak (Matt. 4:1-11), the only weapon He used against the temptations was the Word of God. After three unsuccessful attempts to lure Jesus into sin, and Jesus' faithful response from Scripture, the devil left Him. There's a huge lesson here. If the Son of God used only the Word of God to defeat the enemy of God, how can we possibly think anything else we try (i.e. on our own strength) could have any success? Oh yeah, there's one other prerequisite. We have to have a personal relationship with the Lord Jesus Christ.

In Acts 19:13-16, some Jewish exorcists, 7 sons of Sceva a Jewish chief priest, tried to use the names of Jesus and Paul to cast out a demon. But because they were not Apostles or even believers in Jesus, the demon, still in the man, mocked them and then *"leaped on them and subdued all of them so that they fled out of the house naked and wounded* (v16)." This is a warning we need to take seriously. Spiritual warfare is real. Our enemy is real and has real power. Just not enough to overcome the power inherent in the Word of God.

We're told, *"If any of you lacks wisdom, let him ask of God who gives to all generously and without reproach, and it will be given to him."* (James 1:5). Where does this wisdom come from? *The fear of the Lord is the beginning of wisdom* (Prov. 1:7). *"...the testimony of the Lord is sure, **making wise the simple**"* (Ps. 19:7). So, it's a one-two punch. 1) **Fear the Lord** (know Him, love Him, honor Him through obedience) and 2) **study His "testimony"** (His Word). Don't be an easy target for Satan's lies. Know the truth…it will set you free (John 8:32). *"Be diligent to present yourself approved to God as a workman who does not need to be ashamed, accurately handling the word of truth* (2 Tim. 2:15). The battle is about to get intense as I believe Satan knows his time is short. Keep your sword sharp. Thanks for dropping in. See you in the arena.

*Pastor Al Pittman (In a sermon 4/18/21)

April 23, 2021

You Be the Judge

Is "Santa" an anagram for "Satan?" Is it just a typo or something far more diabolical? We're in a courtroom and the evidence is about to be presented. As in all jury instructions, we are to keep an open mind until we have seen the evidence. In our courtroom, there is one difference. There is no defense, only a presentation of the charges.

Let's start with the purpose(s) of Santa/Satan. Sure it's a commercialized holiday. Stores make a large percentage of their annual sales during the three months prior to Christmas. And, of course, homes are decorated, trees adorned, lights put up and we all ooh and aah. But I believe the **primary purpose** is to distract from the true meaning, the eternal importance of Christmas. To put it simply, Jesus' birth was the opening act in God's plan of salvation. Anything that defocuses our attention from that is a lie from the pit. But it doesn't stop there.

Another purpose of Santa/Satan is to feed our selfishness and greed. We could aptly be named the "Me Generation." We count the presents under the tree. We expect our employers to pony up a bonus while our output typically wanes because of the "Christmas" spirit in the office or workplace. Just look at the kids' faces as you sit around the tree waiting for the presents to be handed out and you'll see anything but a holy respect for the birthday party of our Lord. Further evidence can be found in our comparison to what others got. Did they get more, or more expensive than I? And what feelings are fostered from this comparison? Either pride because we got the "more" end of the stick or envy, maybe anger because we didn't. Both are wrong.

One more piece of evidence not often talked about is how some parents try to make up for a year of poor parenting by spending money they don't have on shiny objects that aren't needed and by New Years will be tucked away in a closet rarely to be seen or used again. Moreover, getting kids to believe in Santa, the Easter Bunny, the tooth fairy, or any other seemingly harmless childhood tradition and then taking it away amounts to lying and then telling the truth and bursting their bubble. It paves the way for this same expectation when trying to get them to believe in God. If that isn't a perversion of God's intent, I can't think of one. And who is it that perverts *everything* from God, the "giver of every perfect gift (Jas. 1:17)"?

Let's face it. For the most part, Christmas is a pagan holiday celebrated by pagans and Christians alike. That's the sad state of the church today. The Bible has a clear warning from God, *"Therefore, come out from their midst and be separate,"* says the Lord. *"and do not touch what is unclean; and I will welcome you."* (2 Cor. 6:17; Isa. 52:11).

I am not advocating totally abandoning traditional Christmas trappings. But I am calling those of us who know the Lord Jesus Christ as our Savior, to hear the message of the Lord to the church at Ephesus in Revelation 2: *"But I have this against you, that you have left your first love."* To finish this section in Revelation, He wraps it up with this, *"He who has an ear, let him hear what the Spirit says to the churches."* (v.7). Are you listening? Do we have a vision of Jesus' glory that transcends all else and pulls us toward the eternity He has planned for us? Do we praise God for who He is as much or more than for what He's done for us?

Friends, I believe the church is on a slippery slope and gathering speed. We have embraced all kinds of Biblical prohibitions from ear-tickling messages to blatant immorality. Yes, thank God there are still godly men in some pulpits and they are not afraid to preach the truth. But they are an endangered species. Satan's mission is obvious, *"The thief* [Satan] *comes only to steal and kill and destroy...*(John 10:10a). Thankfully, there is a part 'b' to this verse, *"I* [Jesus] *came that they may have life, and have it abundantly."*

So it's time to weigh the evidence. Two questions to ask yourself, "1. What does the (worldly) celebration of Christmas—with all its glitter and busyness—do to point me to the One whose birthday we are supposed to be remembering?" There are only two teams to play on. If one of them isn't pointing us to Christ, it has to be "the other one, Santa/Satan, hmm." And then ask, "2. What am I going to do about it?"

April 27, 2021

What if…What Then?

Two posts ago, I talked about the "if, then(s)" in Scripture. For you computer programmers, you understand the relationship. **If** I hit a specific key, **then** a specific response will happen…every time. It's how all software works. It also plays a role in our everyday life. **If** I flip the switch, **then** the lights come on. When the if-then(s) of life don't work the way they should, we know we have a problem. I submit that it's no different in the spiritual realm. And it works both for God and us. In Genesis 18, Abraham was negotiating with God over the destruction of Sodom. God told Abraham, "**If** I find 50 righteous, **then** I will not destroy the city (v.26)." Condition—promise.

Sometimes, the if-then is implied, as in Ps. 84:11, "…*no good thing does He withhold from those who walk uprightly.*" **If** we walk uprightly (condition), **then** He withholds no good thing from us (promise). The Bible is filled with promises from God that have this conditional element (if-then).

Are you struggling with trusting God because you think He's not listening to your prayers? I suggest you examine your adherence to the "if(s)" before you blame God. Here's the best part. The promises—what God will do—are all spelled out for us, along with the "if." Seems like a simple decision. **If** I want the promised blessing, **then** I choose to meet the condition. Here are a couple examples.

Remember God's discussion with Pharoah (through Moses)? "*If you refuse to let them go* (condition), [**then**] *behold, I will smite your whole territory with frogs. (promise)*" (Ex. 8:2). What happened. Frogs everywhere.

If you are looking to know God more, to understand His ways, to increase in wisdom, **then** Proverbs 2 has a great promise, "*(v.1) If you will receive my words and treasure my commandments within you, (v.2) make your ear attentive to wisdom, incline your heart to understanding; (v.3) If you cry for discernment, lift your voice for understanding; (v.4) If you seek her as silver and search for her as for hidden treasures; (v.5) Then you will discern the fear of the Lord and discover the knowledge of God…(v.9) Then you will discern righteousness and justice and equity and every good course, For wisdom* *will enter your heart...*" What is the basic "if" clause here? How do we "receive [God's] words, treasure [God's] commandments?" We MUST renew our minds as Paul wrote to the Romans (12:2). We must spend time in God's word reading, meditating, memorizing, so when we speak, the good treasure in our heart is what comes out (Matt. 12:34,35).

I didn't say it would be easy, but is anything that is valuable and worthwhile? Name one other thing that'll survive the coming destruction of earth besides the Word of God. That's a clue as to the value God places on His Word. The Proverbs 2 verses above liken our mind-renewal to searching for gold, silver, and hidden treasure.

Why spend so much time on this? Many of us blame God for our circumstances when we should accept responsibility for our own laziness and poor choices. We're like the Israelites who constantly grumbled after their release from Egypt. If you read about them, you'll find that they rejected God's rules, turned their back on Him, embraced other gods, and generally thumbed their collective noses at their rescuer, their provider and protector. Can you blame God?

Often, we allow the "good" in life to consume us rather than working through the "better" and persevering all the way to the "best." For those of us who call Christ Savior and friend, the devil is happy to distract us from the narrow path and get us to camp out at the "good," knowing that our witness, our ministry to others is most effective when we strive for the "best." He knows he can't take our salvation, but if he can sideline us, it's as close to a win as he can get.

If we want a closer relationship with our Father, His Word is the answer: "*Establish Your Word to Your servant as that which produces reverence for You*" (Ps. 119:38). I can't say it any plainer. You want to grow in your faith, know your Father better, trust Him for everything in your life, you have to spend time with Him in His Word and prayer.

This is meant as an encouragement to focus on the only truth we can build our lives on. Some of you may take it as judgmental. That's probably the Holy Spirit convicting you, calling you to stay on the narrow path and press on to the "best." Come up with a list of Biblical if-then(s) and see if that helps your understanding. Thanks for reading.

April 29, 2021

Trust the Cure

Fake news. Moving goalposts. Wear masks don't wear masks. How can we believe anything in the media these days when the only constant is change? If masks work, why do we need social distancing? If social distancing works, why do we need masks? Suspicion, distrust, even paranoia are growing with each passing news day. Fear seems to be the driving force behind it all. Ask yourself, what's driving the fear? Who's responsible? We'll get to that in a minute. Vaccinations may or may not work with or without side effects. But first, here's a thought about man's mindset in general. Nobody is interested in a "cure," until they get a "disease." What a great segue into a discussion about man's greatest disease: sin.

The Bible says, *"For **all** have sinned and fall short of the glory of God."* (Rom. 3:23). If ever there was a need for a cure for sin, it's in the 21st century. Everywhere we look, there are growing signs of it in rebellion, rioting, violence, destruction to property, self-centeredness and much more. It sounds like Peter and Paul were writing to our generation, *"Know this first of all, that **in the last days** mockers will come with their mocking, **following after their own lusts**..."* (2 Pet. 3:3). And Paul, *"...**in the last days difficult times will come**. For men will be lovers of self, lovers of money, boastful, arrogant, revilers, disobedient to parents, ungrateful, unholy, unloving, irreconcilable, malicious gossips, without self-control, brutal, haters of good, treacherous, reckless, conceited, lovers of pleasure rather than lovers of God..."* (2 Tim. 3:1-4) Did he miss anything?

The disease is sin. The symptoms are those written above and they have spread worldwide. Fortunately, there is a cure that is 100% certain, available to everyone, has only good side effects, and doesn't cost a dime. Unfortunately, the (temporary) ruler of this world has blinded the eyes of many through distractions, and outright lies disguised as legitimate goals, e.g. "You can have it all" or "of course you deserve it." And, by the way, he [the devil] is the one fanning the flames of fear. When people are afraid and have no anchor to mitigate the fear, they are easily controlled. If you doubt that, ask yourself why people wear masks when alone in their car or walking along the beach.

Contrast that with what the ruler of the universe says in His word. Over 100 times the phrases fear not, do not fear, or do not be afraid appear in Scripture. God does not want us afraid…of COVID-19 or anything else. When we've got the cure for sin, the biggest fear we could ever face—eternity in hell—no longer has any control over us because our future has been secured by Jesus' death and resurrection and by being sealed in Christ with the Holy Spirit of promise. That's a big deal because God's promises never fail.

If, as Peter and Paul have written, we are in the last days and you haven't answered the question of where you'll spend eternity, may I be blunt? Don't wait another day to deliberate. Nobody is promised tomorrow. The Bible says, *"Behold, now is the acceptable time, behold, now is the day of salvation."* (2 Cor.6:2) There IS an afterlife and there are only TWO destinations: heaven and hell. The Bible says, *"…it is appointed for men to die once and **after this** comes judgment."* (Heb. 9:27) Everyone **will be** in one place or the other. Permit one description of each. **In heaven**: *"In* [God's] *presence is fullness of joy, in* [God's] *right hand there are pleasures forever.* (Ps. 16:11). **In hell**: *"…outer darkness, in that place will be weeping and gnashing of teeth."* (Matt. 8:12). Doesn't seem like a hard choice to me. But there are many reasons most won't choose heaven. I don't have space to go into them here, but elsewhere in this book you'll find more information.

Please take this seriously. The disease of **sin is eternally deadly 100% of the time** for those who don't know Jesus Christ as the only cure. Don't be misled by religions that teach you can get there (heaven) by good works or being a "good" person. The Bible says that our good deeds are as "filthy garments" (Isa. 64:6). The requirement for entering heaven is perfection (Matt. 5:48). If you've **ever** lied, stolen, lusted, hated, and more, even once, you've missed the mark.

If you're not sure of your final destination, visit our *"Steps to Salvation"* Appendix. There **you'll get God's perspective on you** and the prescription for the only cure for sin: Jesus Christ. Jesus said, *"I am **the** [only] way and **the** [only] truth and **the** [only] life, no **one** comes to the Father but through Me."* (John 14:6).

April 30, 2021

Biblical Literacy

Four posts ago, we talked about Biblical *Illiteracy*. Today is the other side of the coin. There may be some overlap, but in "illiteracy" we saw that it was self-inflicted due to lack of study, lack of desire, and lack of love for the Father. Today, we'll define "literacy" as knowing the difference between right and wrong, based, not on man's opinions or so-called worldly knowledge, but solely on God's Word.

Standards are the bedrock of society. There are socially acceptable standards (though not acceptable to all). There is the expectation of product consistency (that's why a Big Mac tastes the same in Phoenix, Paris, or Prague). There's even a government department (Commerce) responsible for weights and measures. We need standards. Otherwise chaos would rule.

But all *these* standards are subject to change; some, it seems, are changing before our eyes as society slips further into the darkness of greed, sexual perversion, and self-centeredness. For comparison, look back just 70 years or less to the 50s and 60s. If JFK were alive today, he'd be considered conservative. If we, as a society, were all following the same standards, we wouldn't have the political divide we have. We'd know that guns don't kill people, people do. We'd know that unborn babies are people too. We'd have national pride in our flag, our freedoms, our rule of law. But, alas, that ship has sailed. We will never go back. It's the second law of thermodynamics: the state of entropy (*lack of order or predictability; gradual decline into disorder*) is **irreversible** and will always increase (get worse) over time.

So, do we throw up our hands and surrender to it? If it feels good, do it? That seems to be where we are heading. And apart from Divine intervention, as Barry McGuire sang (1965), "we're on the eve of destruction." It may already be too late. Our God is patient and merciful. But He has set an expiration date at which time, He'll call an end to His waiting and judgment will begin.

This is a wakeup call to those of us who know God and call Jesus Lord. Here are a couple verses to ponder:

Prov. 12:2 *"A **good man** will obtain favor from the Lord, but He will **condemn a man** who **devises evil**."*

Isa. 5:20 "*Woe to those who call evil good, and good evil…*"

Heb. 5:14 "*… **the mature**, who because of practice have their senses **trained to discern good and evil**.*"

3 John 1:11 "*The one who **does good** is of God, the one who **does evil** has not seen God.*"

If we are mature in the Lord, and spend time in God's Word, we should be able to discern good and evil. That's a benefit that unbelievers don't have. They follow their feelings, which can lie to them, instead of God's Word which NEVER lies. We are equipped and armed by the very Spirit of God who wrote the Bible for us to read, study, and understand so that we would be prepared for the battle He knew was coming.

We can see the deterioration of society, the fear that is driving our reactions, and the desperate cry of those seeking answers as to what is going on. Brothers and sisters, we have THE answer: faith in the Lord Jesus Christ. We just need the compassion for lost souls to share it. The Bible says, "*…to one who knows the right thing to do and does not do it, to him it is sin (Jas.4:17).*" And, "*…he who is wise wins souls (Prov. 11:30).*

We're equipped with the "sword," we're wise, the "fields are white for harvest" (John 4:35), and Jesus is coming back soon. My question is simply, do we want to be those of whom Jesus said, "*Blessed is that slave whom his master finds so doing when he comes (Luke 12:43)*"?

May 4, 2021

The FUD Factor

Fear. Uncertainty. Doubt. These are often seeds sown by salesmen who try to denigrate their competitors' products rather than focusing on their own product's advantages. Customers buy because of the FAB (features, advantages, and benefits) of a product, not the negatives of the competition. There is another who sows these same seeds, and, in effect, is trying to sell his product. The devil is the quintessential salesman. His product? The life of least resistance, the easy way with NO restrictions. How's that going for him? If he were paid for spreading fear, he'd be a gazillionaire. Ask yourself, "Do I see fear, uncertainty and doubt all around me today?" If we're honest, we have to say that it's everywhere, it has permeated society.

On the list of top 100 fears (fearof.net) at #12 is thanatophobia—the fear of death and dying, at #27 xenophobia—the fear of the unknown (although current common usage has minimalized the definition to fear of strangers), at #31 theophobia—the fear of God, and at #85 chronophobia—the fear of the future. I find two curiosities in this list of fears. First, that death, the unknown, and the future are not closer together because of the obvious connection; and second, there is the fear of God but no mention of fear of the devil or demons. Another great sales job by the devil. Someone has said the devil's greatest success has been to convince people he doesn't exist.

That's why we should base our lives solely on the inspired Word of God, which never lies, stretches the truth, deceives us, or misleads us but clearly describes our enemy and his ploys. He is a liar, the father of lies (Jn. 8:44). His goal is to steal, kill and destroy (Jn. 10:10) and enslave us to shiny objects and worldly pursuits. As always, Hebrews 2:14, 15 has God's solution, "...*through death He* [Jesus Christ] *might render powerless him who had the power of death, that is, the devil, and might free those who through **fear of death** were **subject to slavery** all their lives.*"

If Christ's death and resurrection rendered the devil powerless, why are so many still slaves of fear? I find it interesting that there even is a list of the top 100 fears, implying there may be many more that didn't make it. God has implanted in every one of us a kind of fear for our protection. We've all heard of the fight or flight response when confronted with danger. We assess, we weigh the options and chance of success with each, then we decide. Phobias, on the other hand, are "exaggerated usually inexplicable and irrational fear of a particular object, class of objects, or situation" (Webster's). Over 100 times, God tells us not to be afraid, and he offers "the peace of God which surpasses all comprehension" (Phil. 4:7). Satan offers "weeds" (Matt. 13: 27, 28, 39).

When we fear, we are not trusting God's Word, *"There is no fear in love; but perfect love casts out fear…(I Jn. 4:18)"* God's Word is the answer to fear of death, the unknown, and the future. We who know Jesus, know the future: WE WIN. Jesus told us to "*…be of good cheer, I have overcome the world* (Jn. 16:33)." We are not to fear the world, current political systems, or where it's all heading. Evil is having its day now, but it's all within God's plan to bring sinners to Himself. Are we about our Father's business of making disciples? While we still have breath, that should be our main focus in ever-expanding concentric circles. First, our family. Then friends, neighbors, and co-workers. Then the world.

Rather than subscribe to the rampant and wide-spread fear prevalent in our country, we need to pray for our leaders in government. Remember, *they* are not the enemy. The enemy has blinded their eyes from seeing and their hearts from desiring the truth. But prayer can change hearts and many times in Scripture, God uses just one man, not a committee.

If you're still a little shaky on your future, hear what Paul says to his readers, *"For to me, to live is Christ and to **die is gain…**having the desire to depart and be with Christ, **for that is very much better** (Phil. 1:21,23)."* That sounds like death is not a jail sentence but Disneyland on steroids…only infinitely better. **The only reason to fear death is if you don't know where you're going after you die.** Many of the pages in this book define the afterlife thoroughly, so I won't repeat it here. But if you'd like to know more, go directly to the Appendix: *Steps to Salvation*. The answer to ALL your fears is found in a relationship with Jesus Christ. Thanks for stopping in.

May 9, 2021

Listen Up

Can You Hear? God is speaking to you…through His creation and His Word. Be quiet. Unplug. You'll hear it. Let me start by saying that nobody can *prove* God exists. But I submit that the evidence is over-whelming for His existence, and only a *"worthless person, a wicked man"* (Prov. 6:12) would deny the obvious. There are many reasons for denial, but the one that jumps out at me is that he doesn't believe the consequences of not knowing God. Here's the rest of the section in Proverbs: v.15, *"his* [Bob's] *calamity will come suddenly; instantly he will be broken and there will be NO healing."* Wow.

Whether this applies to Bob's earthly or eternal life, the finality of the sentencing should literally scare hell out of him. Hell is real. Time is short before Jesus returns for His church (those who trust Him for salvation) to take us to heaven. There's no way words like calamity, broken, and no healing, can convey a warm, embracing feeling. More likely fear. We dealt with that in our last post. It's everywhere. We saw that only a relationship to Jesus can release anyone from their fear. But that's not the point of this discussion.

In Psalm 19, the psalmist starts out with, v.1 *"The heavens are* **telling** *of the glory of God and their expanse is* **declaring** *the work of His hands."* Everybody sees the heavens. By day, the sun illumines and warms. Science has shown that 93 million miles is the exact distance needed to keep the earth from burning to a crisp or becoming a popsicle. By night, the beauty of billions of stars, just in the Milky Way, provide an unparalleled light show. But that's only the start.

Romans 1:18-22 says, *"For the wrath of God is revealed from heaven against all ungodliness and unrighteousness of **men who sup-press the truth** in unrighteousness, because **that which is known about God is evident within them**; for God made it evident to them. For since ... creation ... **His invisible attributes, His eternal power** and **divine nature**, have been **clearly seen**, being **understood through what has been made, so that they are without excuse**. For even though they knew God, they did not honor Him as God or give thanks, but **they became futile** in their speculations, and their foolish heart was darkened. **Professing to be wise, they became fools**…*

We see with our own eyes and marvel at the magnificence of God's creation. And we hear from God's Spirit that the creation announces God's invisible attributes and power. But there's also the Bible, literally the best-selling book of all time. According to The Guinness Book of World Records in 1995, over 5 billion copies of the Bible had been sold. Here's one reason, *"For the Word of God is living and active and sharper than any two-edged sword...able to judge the thoughts and intentions of the heart* (Heb. 4:12)."

So, in case you missed God's glory in His creation, you can't miss it in His Word. His character qualities of love, mercy, patience, and so many more are on every page. I like to call it "the owner's manual," you know, the how-to book that accompanies a new product. If we're in Christ, we are new products (creatures) (2 Cor. 5:17). Read the manual. You'll find all kinds of how-to information from prayer to perseverance, accountability to faithfulness, literally everything necessary for living righteously in an unrighteous world.

What is the "noise" that's keeping you from hearing God's creation? Is it literal noise like constantly plugged-in devices? Or is it the noise of busyness which is often a symptom of avoidance? What are you afraid of? Do you know there *is* a God and that He can't tolerate sin, and you also know that *you're* a sinner and are afraid of His judgment?

I've got **great news** for you. You don't have to be afraid, no matter how bad you think your sin is, God's grace and mercy are greater. Listen to God's invitation to YOU: *"'Come now, and let us reason together' says the Lord, 'though your sins are as scarlet, they will be as white as snow...* (Isa. 1:18).'" How, you ask yourself, can my blackness of sin become white as snow? You're right. There is a price for sin. The Bible says, *"...the wages of sin is death, but the **free gift of God** is eternal life in Christ Jesus our Lord* (Rom. 6:23)." But the price was paid on your behalf by Jesus' death and resurrection. You just have to acknowledge that you are a sinner and can't come up with anything (good deeds, charitable donations, nothing) to save yourself, and that you believe what Jesus said about Himself, *"I am the way and the truth and the life, no one comes to the Father but through Me* (John 14:6)." To have a relationship with the Creator of the universe and His Son, visit Appendix: *"Steps to Salvation"* in the back of this book.

June 1, 2021

Is Fear King

On Sunday, May 16th, Pastor Al said this, "Hopelessness abounds in America today because fear is king." Before we unpack that, consider a couple questions. Is fear prevalent across all age categories? Both sexes? Christians and non-Christians? How can we eliminate this hopelessness?

The answer to the first three is absolutely yes. We'll get to the last one in a minute. I understand the fear raging across America. But I don't buy into it. We've seen "science" bounce all over. One day, masks. The next, no masks. Then they're back again. Children, it's been proven, who have a low susceptibility to the virus, and are not likely to be carriers, were forced to quarantine and do school via computer, which proved to have a more negative impact vis-à-vis poor learning and higher suicide rates than potentially being exposed to the virus. And we can't forget the poor teachers (and their unions), who seem to care only for additional pay and benefits rather than the children who are falling behind. It's all about who has the control, a powerful, addictive aphrodisiac sought by many.

One other line of thinking that really bothers me, for which I have yet to hear a reasonable explanation: If the vaccines are so safe, why is there such pressure to get them, and why all the "incentives" to put a "gene modifier" (mRNA) into our bodies. What happened to "the better mousetrap"? And "If you build it, they will come." Who profits from all this? And why are scientists, Like Dr. Sherri Tenpenny who offers reasonable, if not conclusive evidence, censored from mainstream media?

But lest I go too far down the rabbit hole, let's look at fear itself. What causes it? Is it logical, rational, controllable? If you analyze it, irrational fear occurs about 85% of the time over things that never happen. And "the stress hormones that worry dumps into our brains have been linked to shrinking brain mass, lowering our IQ, being prone to heart disease, cancer, and premature aging, clinical depression, and making seniors more likely to develop dementia and Alzheimer's." (Unsubstantiated quote from Don Joseph Goewey, author of "*The End of Stress*.").

Some fear is good. God gave each of us a "fight or flight" response to danger. It is right to fear immediate or foreseeable danger. Not so much, things that *might* happen. Yes, of course, we are to utilize the "wisdom from above" in our daily living. But fear of the unknown, for example, belongs in the 85% category. Especially if we know who holds the future and trust Him to "have our six." And therein lies the answer to our 4th question: How do we eliminate this hopelessness?

As believers in Jesus Christ, you and I—the church—are told many times to "fear not." Why? Because God is on His throne and still rules the universe. Nothing happens outside His perfect plan for us individually and for the world at large. So, first of all, fear is disobedience. Secondly, the church is to be salt and light in a lost world, a culture of global fear. We have the ONLY answer to the "hopelessness" question. But if our words are no different than the world's, and our message, as heard in our actions, is a carbon copy of the world's, why would anybody listen to us?

Wake up church. WE HAVE THE ANSWER: Jesus Christ is the ONE TRUE SOURCE of hope. "*The fear of the Lord is the **beginning** of wisdom; a good understanding have all those who **DO** His commandments.*" (Ps. 111:10). God is calling His church to be ready for battle. Our enemy is not the political system (although he uses it against us), it's not any form of flesh and blood (although we focus on that which we see). No, it's the "prince of the power of the air" (Eph. 2:2). "*Do not fear those who kill the body but are unable to kill the soul: but rather fear Him who is able to destroy both soul and body in hell*" (Matt. 10:28). I encourage you to read the end of His-story. WE WIN regardless of what it looks like now. Someone has said, rather than fear the darkness, light a candle.

If you're a believer and are burdened with fear, how much time are you spending in God's word and prayer? How well do you really know the character of God? He CANNOT lie. Therefore, everything you read in His word is the truth on which you can base your life, your hope, and your future. Dig in. You can never devour too much truth.

If you're not a believer and are burdened with fear, you need to know that the God of the universe knows you, loves you, sent His son Jesus to die in your stead just so you could have a relationship with Him. If that doesn't give you hope, check your pulse. For more specific information about how you can know this God, visit our *Steps to Salvation* Appendix in the back of this book. Thanks for dropping in. Hope is waiting to overwhelm you by God's goodness and mercy. Don't wait another day.

June 11, 2021

Prepare For The Storm

What storm? Well, pick one. If you believe in global warming and all the predictions from the "scientists," we're in for increased hurricane activity, tornados, and firestorms. The polar icecaps are going to melt and raise the ocean levels. But if you read our last post, *Is Fear King*, you'll realize it's just more of "their" scare tactics to keep us bound in fear.

There is, however, a storm coming for which we *can* and *should* prepare. It will come when least expected. There will be no further warnings or telltale signs other than the depravity of man continuing the downward spiral. Not being prepared will introduce us to the worst nightmare imaginable on a global scale. And there will be no place to hide from it nor will we awaken out of it. No, I'm not talking about a fresh outbreak of COVID-19 (24, 57 or whatever), although that could be a part of it. And natural disasters will destroy much of the world, although there will be nothing "natural" about them.

We are, and have been for decades, on a slippery slope of immorality and self-centeredness the likes of which might have only existed before "The Flood," in which the entire earth's population, less eight people, was destroyed. The problem is, like the frog in the pot of water, our environment has changed so slowly, we haven't recognized it because what should have been the standard, the benchmark, has changed along with it. We are about to boil to death, and it feels normal.

Though the God who created everything, and sustains it with His word, is singularly patient and loving, He has a timetable that, I believe, is rapidly approaching expiration. If that's true, how do we prepare? Is there any way to avoid it?

For a typical storm, there are two types of preparation necessary: physical and mental. For *this* one, neither will help. We must be prepared *spiritually*. And only those who are, *will* escape. In I Peter 1:13, we're told to "***prepare your minds for action***, *keep sober in spirit, fix your hope completely on the grace to be brought to you at the revelation of Jesus Christ.*" How do we prepare our minds? Romans 12:2 has the answer, "*And **do not be conformed to this world***, *but be* *transformed by the **renewing of your mind**, so that you may prove what the will of God is, that which is good and acceptable and perfect."* We can only do that when we are "new creatures." II Corinthians 5:17 says, *"...**if anyone is in Christ, he is a new creature**, the old things passed away; behold, new things have come."*

The *only* prerequisite to be included in the group that escapes the coming storm is to know Jesus Christ personally as your Savior and Lord. If you do, you're in. If not, you're out. Period. End of story. But it's a story with a happy ending...if you "renew your mind" and become a "new creation."

Fortunately, it's not a long arduous transformation. It can happen instantly when you 1) agree with God that you're a sinner, separated from Him (Rom. 3:23) and deserving of death (Rom. 6:23), 2) realize there's nothing *you* can do to restore the relationship, except repent of your sin (tell God you're sorry) and ask for forgiveness based on Jesus Christ's death on your behalf (John 14:6), 3) accept God's *free gift* of salvation (Eph. 2:8,9).

Escaping the coming storm (judgment) is just the beginning. Heaven awaits and it will be glorious. There will be no sin there...ever. No sorrow, no pain, no death, bitterness, envy, lying, stealing or any other negative thing you can think of. Just the glory of God and Jesus our Savior. We'll see the angels who are magnificent, created beings. We'll walk on streets of gold. Each of the twelve gates in the New Jerusalem is a single pearl. Satan and his demons, who have tormented us and sought our destruction during our time on earth, will have been banished to the never-ending fires of hell that burn for eternity. Now that's something to look forward to.

Check out our *"Steps To Salvation"* Appendix in the back of this book for more detailed information about becoming a new creature, prepared for the coming storm.

August 6, 2021

You Follow Me

Anyone ever ask you, "How do I know God's will for me?" Do you have a good answer? You know, one of the things I love about the Bible is its simplicity. Jesus chose twelve "uneducated" men to evangelize the world. Why do you suppose that was? Simple answer: "...*Has not God made foolish the wisdom of the world?*" (I Cor. 1:20); "*Because the foolishness of God is wiser than men...*" (I Cor. 1:25). Look around. I'm sure you could name well-educated people who lack common sense, whose ideas of truth are 180 degrees out of sync with reality. The twelve He chose didn't have to be un-taught to learn truth.

Besides being simple, the Bible is crystal clear on many subjects. When Jesus had something to say, He said it so anybody open to the truth could grasp it. For example, when Jesus was talking about heaven and Thomas asked him the way, his answer was, wait for it…simple: "*I am the way and the truth and the life, no one comes to the Father but through Me.*" (John 14:6). Can't get much plainer than that. But why do so many miss that truth? It has to do with the prerequisite: going through the right "Gate." This Gate requires humility, submission, emptiness of self. Not something many of us are willing to do—even though it's free.

Walking with God is an individual relationship. It's been said that God doesn't have any grandchildren. We can want salvation for others, share the gospel with them, pray for their souls, but the Holy Spirit has to awaken them to their need (of a Savior) and the ONLY solution: Jesus. It's easy to get caught up in comparisons between ourselves and others. We look at jobs, housing, money, positions in church leadership, and other metrics. And we're not the only ones.

Peter, one of Jesus' inner circle, along with James and John, had just received a prophecy from Jesus about how he would die (John 21:18,19). Perhaps out of natural curiosity or something else, he asked about John, "...*Lord, what about this man?*" (v. 21). In modern vernacular, Jesus told Peter it was none of his business (v.22) and then the "simple" truth: "***You follow me!***" (v. 22).

How do we know God's will? It's very simple. Read the Bible and notice God's commands…then do them. Here are just a few: "*You *shall love the Lord your God with all your **heart**, and with all your **soul**, and with all your **mind**, and with all your **strength**."* (Mark 12:30). *"But seek first His kingdom and His righteousness and all these things* [food, drink, clothing] *will be added to you."* (Matt. 6:33). *"Do nothing from selfishness or empty conceit, but with humility of mind regard one another as more important than yourselves; do not merely look out for your own personal interests, but also for the interests of others. "* (Phil. 2:3,4). *"And do not be conformed to this world, but be transformed by the renewing of your mind, so that you may prove what the will of God is..."* (Rom. 12:2).

There are many more commands, including a "list of ten" in Exodus 20. They start with "you shall and you shall not." It's not that we don't **know** God's will. It's that we don't **do** His will. Every one of us is educated beyond our obedience. If we just picked a handful of the Lord's commands and faithfully did them, our lives, our churches, our communities would reflect God's glory in His saints. We'd be irresistible to a lost and dying world. Something to think about when we scratch our heads and wonder what God's will is for our life.

August 20, 2021

Free From the Fear of Death

Our home page says this site (https://needanewplan.com) is filled with good news. Today's post is one example. If you or someone you know is afraid of dying, this post is for you. In *The FUD Factor* (May 4), we said the only reason to fear death is if you don't know where you go after you die.

First, can we agree on some basics? One, everybody dies. Two, nobody knows when they will take their last breath. Three, there is an afterlife. (Some may not believe this point. But, for the sake of argument, assume it's true.) Fourth, there are no second chances. Fifth, we can know positively where we go when we die.

My only proof text is the Bible. If you struggle with its veracity, then you're not likely to be convinced by anything I say. But if you can accept that every word of it is true, then this will make a lot of sense to you. Here we go.

There are many verses that support my position, but I've chosen one that covers most of the points: "*...it is appointed for men to **die once** and **after this comes judgment**...*" (Heb. 9:27). We all die...once. There is no reincarnation, no limbo, no appellate court. God assigned a finite number of days for each of us before we were born, "*...and in Your book were all written the days that were ordained for me, when as yet there was not one of them*" (Ps. 139:16). **After** we die, we stand before God in judgment. If all we have are our good deeds to present as evidence why we should be allowed into heaven, we're in trouble.

The Bible says, "*...**all our righteous deeds are like a filthy garment**"* (Isa. 64:6). Jesus said, "***I am the*** [only] ***way*** *and the truth and the life,* ***no one comes to the Father but through Me***" (John 14:6). If there is "nothing" when we die, what would be the purpose of judgment? We could say, like the rich man in Jesus' parable, "*...soul...eat, drink and be merry*" (Luke 12:19). But God said to him, "*You fool! This very night your soul is required of you*" (v.20).

If there were nothing after we die, Paul's word to the Corinthians would be our legacy, "*If we have hoped in Christ **in this life only**, we are of all men most to be pitied.*" (I Cor. 15:19). But pity is NOT our legacy. HOPE is. The writer of Hebrews places an exclamation mark on this hope, "*...that through death He (Christ) might render powerless him who had the power of death, that is, the devil, and might **free those who through fear of death** were subject to slavery all their lives.*" (Heb. 2:14,15).

The past 18 months have been filled with racial tension, people and groups fanning the flames of hatred, and lots of references to slavery. The truth is, we're all slaves to something. "*Do you not know...**you are slaves of the one whom you obey**, either of **sin resulting in death**, or of **obedience resulting in righteousness?**" (Rom. 6:16) There are **only two camps**, a **conscious choice** of righteousness, or the **default** of sin. One leads to heaven, the other to hell.

That covers the first four. Let's end with the most important one: You can **know positively** where you'll spend eternity. John 14:6 tells us that **Jesus** is the **only way to God**. Good deeds, or works, as we've seen, won't do it. Church attendance, baptism, money, volunteering for good causes all fall into the category of "works," none of which is acceptable payment of the entry fee to heaven. The standard that God accepts is perfection—not one single sin our whole life. Impossible? For us, yes. But Jesus came to earth as a flesh and blood man, lived a perfect life, then died to pay the price—the entrance fee to heaven— for all men who come to Him in humility and repentance. He said, "*...the one who comes to Me I will **certainly** not cast out (John 6:37).*" That's a promise for anyone.

If you're a believer in Jesus Christ and you fear death, take time to ponder this post. Look up the scripture verses. Ask the Holy Spirit to give you understanding and meditate on the following promises of God. "*Therefore there is now **no condemnation** for those who are in Christ Jesus.*" Rom. 8:1 "*If we confess our sins, **He is faithful** and righteous **to forgive** us our sins and to cleanse us from **all** unrighteousness.*" I Jn. 1:9 "*These things I have written to you who believe in the name of the Son of God, so that **you may know** that **you have eternal life**.*" I Jn. 5:13

If you're not sure about all this, it could be that you don't know Jesus personally. We have an Appendix, *Steps to Salvation,* that goes into a more detailed explanation of how you can know for sure that you'll go to heaven when you die. Once that question is settled, the fear of the future, the unknown and your final destination will be replaced with confidence and a joyous expectation of meeting Jesus face to face. Thanks for reading.

September 9, 2021

Hope Does Not Disappoint... if it's in the right thing.

"...we exult in our tribulations, knowing that tribulation brings about perseverance; and perseverance, proven character; and proven character, hope; and **hope does not disappoint, because** *the love of God has been poured out within our hearts..."* (Rom. 5:3-5)

We are living in a time of hopelessness. Pandemics and politicians have painted pictures of doom and gloom wrapped in a cloak of resolution and abandonment. Misery is the new normal. "Natural" disasters—floods, fires, and the like—coupled with humanity's selfishness and evil behavior toward each other, have monopolized the news media for months.

It's been said that we are what we eat. If all we're consuming is a steady diet of negativism and lies from the Fourth Estate, we're bound to show signs of malnutrition in our thinking and beliefs. Hope in science (and scientists), politics (and politicians), or "the innate goodness of mankind," leads to nothing but more hopelessness. Intuitively, you know that to be so from personal experience. In the last 18 months, science has been so distorted by "scientists" as to not be believable. Politicians lie with impunity. And as for the goodness of mankind, really?

If you've read any of our other posts, you know we write the truth from a Biblical perspective. Anything we put hope in besides a personal relationship with Jesus Christ and the mercy and grace available to all from God the Father cannot deliver anything but disappointment, despair, and disillusionment. That's why, as a society and as individuals, we're in the condition we are. Recognizing a problem is the first step toward a remedy, a change in outcome.

Permit one example. The state of California, where I was born and raised, is in shambles because of bad decisions by leaders for decades. Taxes, unemployment, and homelessness are at or near the worst in the nation. Changing governors through a recall election is only a Band-Aid on the real problem, which is sin. And that's a heart problem, nothing that money or a change of leadership can correct. Until individuals recognize their utter depravity apart from Jesus Christ, nothing will change.

God is patient along with loving, kind, merciful and more. But He has a timetable that's immutable. Sin *will* extract its due: *"all have sinned and fall short of the glory of God."* (Rom. 3:23). *"For the wages of sin is death,"* (Rom 6:23a). But we're a purveyor of good news and if I left it there, it wouldn't be good. So, in the same verse, Paul gives us the answer: *"but the **free gift** of God is eternal life in Christ Jesus our Lord."* (Rom. 6:23b). Free is good, right? You say, "yeah, but it sounds too good to be true."

It's true. God loves you no matter what you've done. But He has a standard of perfection that none of us can attain on our own. Before you think, "What's the use?" there's more good news. Jesus Christ was born for one purpose: to save sinners. He lived a perfect life and paid for our sin by his death on the cross. He rose from the grave and is now seated with His Father in heaven, where He advocates for us with God. What's the catch? There isn't one. But it does cost us something. We have to give up our pride, come to Jesus in humility, admit that we're sinners unable to save ourselves, and throw ourselves on God's mercy. He promised that if we do that, *"...the one who comes to Me I will certainly not cast out."* (John 6:37).

That's a lot to say to get to the message of hope. There's an old hymn that has the line, "My hope is built on nothing less than Jesus' blood and righteousness." That's the source of our hope, the sum of our hope, and the security of our hope. For a little more in-depth look at hope, read our last post *"Free From the Fear of Death."* And if you'd like to know more about how you can have this relationship with Jesus, read our *"Steps to Salvation"* Appendix in the back of the book. Thanks for stopping by.

September 13, 2021

Identity Influences Behavior

I identify as… (fill in the blank). Abraham Lincoln asked, "If you call a dog's tail a leg, how many legs do you have?" You'd be surprised how many people answer five, not four, without even thinking. The other possible answer is two, depending on which word you emphasize (legs or you). During the 2008 presidential election, Barack Obama said, "you can put lipstick on a pig, but it's still a pig" which was taken by an angry McCain campaign as an "out of bounds attack on running mate Sarah Palin." Still, the truth at the heart of the statement stands. Do what you will with a pig, it will always be a pig.

The point is simply that just because you call something by a different name, doesn't make it so. So what does that have to do with our quest for truth? As always, our final arbiter of truth is God's Word which never changes no matter how much current trends attempt to discredit or change meanings or standards.

The Bible is very clear. *"God created man in His own image, in the image of God He created him; male and female He created them."* (Gen. 1:27). Not only was *man* created as male and female, but *all creatures* were too. Six times in Genesis 6 and 7, God reiterates the phrase "male and female" referring to the pairs Noah was to take aboard the ark. Since all of creation, except for eight people (Noah, his wife, his three sons and their wives) and the animals that Noah was told to bring aboard, was about to be destroyed in a worldwide flood, how would the earth be repopulated by man or beast if the natural binary order wasn't adhered to. No matter how much of "nature" is denied, two women can't produce a baby.

Since time began, Satan has tried to thwart God's design for mankind through lies and deception. And man, who rebels against God has been a willing dupe. Consider the latest evil inspired teaching raging across our country in schools: CRT, Critical Race Theory. I'd like to focus on the word "theory." Webster's defines it this way, "a belief, policy, or procedure proposed or followed as the basis of action." In the science community, theories are proposed to spawn discovery of truth. But they are still theories…until proven.

CRT, which has its roots in Marxism, is based solely on race. If you're white, you're an *oppressor*. If you're black or brown, you're *oppressed*. It promotes identity in the color of your skin. As an oppressed person, you are encouraged to adopt a programmed behavior, to act certain ways, demand certain things, and blame others. As an "oppressor" you're guilty of anything and everything creating all the ills endured by the oppressed. Never mind the concepts of hard work and diligence on one hand or bad decisions and choices on the other hand. By the way, if this "theory" is true, we'd have no successful blacks or no down-and-out whites.

The questions is, "Do you identify as what CRT says the color of your skin dictates?" Don't buy the lie. Racism has always been with us. In Biblical times, Jews and the half-breed Samaritans hated each other. In more modern times, slavery was practiced by blacks on blacks as well as by whites on blacks and even whites on whites. But that's not the point. Anyone reading this is not and has not been part of a group systematically oppressed by another group. As much as we might want to blame somebody else for our current condition, we can't.

So how do you identify yourself? Can you be honest? Are you disciplined or lazy? Dedicated or lethargic? Accountable or a blamer? Whatever your current state, you can improve it by a decision. If you know Jesus Christ as your Savior, your identity is **in Christ.** The Bible says, *"There is neither Jew nor Greek, there is neither slave nor free man, there is neither male nor female; for you are all **one in Christ Jesus**."* (Gal. 3:28 emphasis added).

If you don't know Jesus, and you want to, it's not too late. He loves you in spite of your warts. There's nothing you've done that is so bad that He would refuse you. In fact He says, *"...the one who comes to Me I will certainly not cast out."* (John 6:37). What does it mean to "come to Him"? It means to admit your sin has driven a wedge between you and God and on your own, there's nothing you can do to remove that. But Jesus will when you come in humility and tell Him you want to become part of His family. For a more detailed explanation, see the Appendix, "Steps to Salvation" in the back of this book.

For those of us who already know Jesus, our identity is not defined by the world, but by the God who created it. *"If we walk in the Light as He Himself is in the Light, we have fellowship with one another...*" (1 John 1:7). Let's make sure our behavior is consistent with our identity.

October 28, 2021

Blameless with Great Joy

Not guilty! From a simple traffic violation to the grisliest murder, those words spell freedom, release, a second chance. And who in their right mind wouldn't want to hear them? That's why it's so hard to accept the fact that many people will consciously walk away from the ultimate Not Guilty—forgiveness of sins through the blood of Jesus Christ—and remain locked in their prison which carries an automatic and eternal death sentence.

Not guilty doesn't necessarily mean without any hint of culpability. It could be that there just wasn't enough evidence to judge "beyond a reasonable doubt." Blameless with great joy; is a concept found in the Book of Jude, verse 24. But blameless means not only not guilty, it goes beyond that. It implies a clean slate, no sign of an offense, pure, righteous, undefiled. Wow. And then the icing: with great joy.

I've never been in jail so I'm not speaking from experience. But I can imagine some level of joy or relief of hopelessness upon release. The problem with this type of release is the rate of recidivism is high in many states, even those with a large population. So this is temporary at best, even for those not returning to Graybar Hotel.

One big difference between a court-levied sentence and God's pronouncement of guilt is one can be based on flimsy or flawed evidence and you can be convicted though innocent. The other (God's) is perfect judgment because He sees all and knows all; nobody escapes His watchfulness. Because of that and because "all have sinned" (Rom. 3:23) and thus are guilty of God's law, all have earned the death penalty (Rom. 6:23). But we have a defense attorney, an advocate, in Jesus Christ. The Bible says, "...*He always lives to make intercession for them* (those who draw near to God through Jesus), Heb. 7:25. Who better to represent us before the court of God?

Think about one of the most joyous events in your life: perhaps your wedding day, or the birth of a child, or that big promotion you worked so hard for. Whatever amount of joy you felt, it doesn't last very long. But the joy that comes with God's declaration of "blameless," lasts throughout eternity. Words can't do justice to the depth of joy we know because our sins are forgiven. Joy now because we know our future is secure. Jesus said, *"I go to prepare a place for you. If I go and prepare a place for you, I will come again and receive you to Myself, that where I am, there you may be also."* (John 14:2,3), and joy forever because we'll be in Jesus' presence. The psalmist said, *"...in Your presence is fullness of joy"* (Psalm 16:11).

Not just "not guilty," but "blameless." Not just joy, but *great* joy. We can experience both of these now. Jesus said, *"The one who comes to Me, I will certainly not cast out"* (John 6:37). Have you come to Him...on His terms? Forgiveness, resulting in the declaration of blameless, comes only through repenting (turning away from your sin) and believing that you are one of those for whom Jesus died and rose again. There's a complete outline in the Appendix, Steps to Salvation in the back of this book that gives you God's perspective on you and your final destiny. If you're not experiencing the joy of knowing you are blameless in God's eyes, please take a few minutes to visit the page. Thanks for reading.

November 10, 2021

Once in…ever!

Have you ever bet on a football game? A horse race? How do the bookmakers determine what to pay if you win? Part is history, part is potential, other competitors, a lot of subjectivity. And they still are wrong much of the time. Consider the recent Denver Broncos – Dallas Cowboys game (Nov. 7, 2021). Going into the game, the Broncos had a mediocre record at best (4-4) and had beaten mostly weaker teams. While Dallas went into the game with a 6-1 record. Not many thought the Broncos could win in Dallas' home stadium. But they did. Surprise, disbelief, stunned, are some of the words thrown around in the media and locker room chatter.

In life it's said the only sure things are death and taxes. But what about in death? Is there any sure thing? And how do I hedge my bet to improve my odds? There is one event on the horizon that has never happened before. So current odds-making strategies have no precedent. But as sure as we will all die someday, this event will happen and the same words of incredulity—surprise, disbelief, stunned—will be on many lips.

Whether you believe that Jesus Christ is God, you have to admit He is an historic figure. In fact, much of His recorded words are the basis, at least at one time, of many of our laws. For those of us who do believe Jesus is God, His words take on additional weight and meaning because He *cannot* lie (Tit. 1:2). For example, He said, *"…I go to prepare a place for you. If I go and prepare a place for you, I will come again, and receive you to Myself, that where I am, there you may be also* (John 14, 2,3). Just like the worldwide flood that covered the earth and killed all but eight people in Noah's day had never happened before, Jesus' coming back for His church hasn't either. But Peter addresses this too, *"…in the last days mockers will come with their mocking, following after their own lusts, and saying, 'Where is the promise of His coming? For ever since the fathers fell asleep, all continues just as it was from the beginning of creation'"* (2 Pet. 3:3,4). Obviously they didn't know their own history (the flood).

These mockers are with us today. Listen to Paul's warning to Timothy, *"But realize this, that in the last days difficult times will come.*

For men will be lovers of self, lovers of money, boastful, arrogant, revilers, disobedient to parents, ungrateful, unholy, unloving, irreconcilable, malicious gossips, without self-control, brutal, haters of good, treacherous, reckless, conceited, lovers of pleasure rather than lovers of God, holding to a form of godliness, although they have denied its power; Avoid such men as these" (2 Tim. 3:1-5).

If that doesn't describe our current situation, I don't know what it'll take. Listen to Jesus' words to the Pharisees and Sadducees, *"When it is evening, you say, 'It will be fair weather, for the sky is red.' And in the morning, 'There will be a storm today, for the sky is red and threatening.' Do you know how to discern the appearance of the sky, but cannot discern the signs of the times?"* (Matt. 16:2,3). (Bet you didn't know the saying, "Red sky in the morning, sailors take warning. Red sky at night, sailors delight" was taken from the Bible.) Aren't we a lot like Jesus' audience in not recognizing the rapidity with which we are in a downward spiral, spawned and impacted by poor leadership, failing morals, and a general disregard for right and wrong?

Jesus WILL return. Not setting any timetable, that's strictly up to God, who planned the calendar from before the beginning of time. But there won't be any 30-day notice or second chances once the trumpet blows (1 Thess. 4:16,17). The Bible says, *"...it is appointed for men to die once and after this comes judgment"* (Heb. 9:27). My hope for everyone reading this is that you will be ready.

If you're ready to meet God face to face, praise Him. You probably know someone who isn't. Time is short. Get off the bench and into the game. If you're not ready to meet Him or think that you've "been good enough" your future is bleak. Visit our Appendix, "Steps to Salvation". You'll get a good understanding of what God thinks of you and a roadmap to move your odds from zero to 100% of eternity with Jesus in heaven. Hope to see you there.

Thanksgiving

Turkey and pie…oh my oh my
How far we have drifted
From our Creator on high
To think anything good,
Could, would or should
Come from our acts
Apart from the facts
That all that is ours
Whether hovels or towers
Was given in love
By our Father above
To cause giving of thanks
Not trusting in banks
Nor boasting of deeds
Taking credit for seeds
That grow nothing but weeds
While all that we've done,
Blessed by Father and Son,
Is not ours to claim
But points to The name
That heals blind and lame
So we'll know in our heart
We are nothing apart…
From Him.
    Mike Thornton

"For who regards you as superior?
What do you have that you did not receive?
And if you did receive it, why do you boast
as if you had not received it." I Cor. 4:7

December 7, 2021

Rewards or Regrets? *

Jonathan Edwards, a giant of the faith from the 18th century (1703-1758), is said to have asked this question: "What will you wish you had done when you come to die?" It's a very thought-provoking question for both those of us who know Jesus Christ as our Savior and those who don't. The Apostle Paul said it this way in his second letter to the church in Corinth, *"For we must all appear before the judgment seat of Christ, so that each one may be recompensed for his deeds in the body, according to what he has done, whether good or bad"* (II Cor. 5:10). The only judgment seat for believers, whose sin was dealt with at the cross, is the one at which our works and motives are exposed. Everything done with God-honoring motives will be rewarded. All else will be considered "wood, hay, and stubble"—worthless—and burned up.

This verse is NOT teaching that good works get us into heaven. That's obvious from many other verses, such as Eph. 2:8,9, *"For **by grace** you have been saved through faith and that not of yourselves, it is the gift of God, **not as a result of works** so that no one may boast"* (emphasis added). Rather, it is an awakening call reminding us that God watches everything we do and keeps records of it all. If we have accepted Jesus' substitutionary death on our behalf, we are headed for heaven. Period. There is nothing that can separate us from the love of God, which is in Christ Jesus our Lord (Rom. 8:37-39).

But ask yourself this, Wouldn't I rather have the rewards of a righteous life, earned in grateful service to the God who saved me and has prepared a place for me in heaven, than to spend eternity with regrets over things I coulda, shoulda, woulda done while I lived on earth?

I don't know exactly what rewards to expect, but I do know two things. First, Jesus said, *"Behold, I am coming quickly, and My **reward is with Me**, to render **to every man according to what he has done"*** (Rev. 22"12). And second, having experienced and enjoyed God's creative power and amazing beauty and variety of earth's treasures while on earth, whatever He's come up with for rewards has got to be beyond my imagination, and that gets me excited.

So what does all that have to do with today's title? It should create or stir an urgency in us to make sure we get all the rewards we can. Why else would God tell us about rewards if it weren't a good goal? But in that urgency, don't we know family members or friends whose future hasn't been cast in stone yet? Don't we want them to experience "fullness of joy" and "pleasures forever" (Psalm 16:11)?

In God's wisdom, He has given us an opportunity to amass rewards while obeying Jesus' final command to His church, *"Go...make disciples...baptize...teach obedience"* (Matt. 28:19,20). Seems like a no-brainer to me. How about you?

I hope juxtaposing rewards and regrets causes you to ponder deeply the ramifications of what your daily plan and activities are producing for (your) eternity.

*Idea from a message by Dr. Bryan Fields, Grace Chapel Castle Rock, CO

February 3, 2022

Grace and Glory…

As Paul Harvey used to say, "and now…the rest of the story". To-day's title is the start of the Scripture that ends, *"…No good thing does He withhold from those who walk uprightly"* (Psalm 84:11b). If the story ended at the title, we'd be looking at the future only for those who know Jesus as their Savior. But praise God, it *doesn't* end there for those of us who *don't* know Him.

Easter is coming and I can't think of a better way to prepare for that day—which began as a day of extreme sadness because the disciples' friend and teacher, who had been inseparable from them for three years, had been murdered three days ago before their very eyes. In their ignorance, they didn't understand what was happening. They couldn't have possibly been more sad, more discouraged, lonelier. But they were in for the biggest surprise of their lives. Jesus was alive! Unlike during The Tribulation when people give gifts to each other because of the death of the two prophets of God (Rev. 11:10), at Easter, God gives us the infinitely costly gift of eternal life with Him, all at no cost to us…FREE.

We tend to think of Christmas as the time for gift-giving. But it was just the beginning, chapter one, if you will. Easter is the final chapter of God's "I told you so" love letter to the world. The *best* gift ever: salvation through The Lord Jesus Christ. What does Easter mean to the family of God? To begin with, our sins are forgiven and our relationship with our heavenly Father is re-established. That means we are now in line for every promise of God. Let's look at the big picture and one of my favorite promises, a home in heaven with Jesus. Jesus promised, *"I go to prepare a place for you. If I go and prepare a place for you, I will come again and receive you to Myself, that where I am, there you may be also"* (John 14,2b, 3).

Why is that so special? The psalmist answers: *"…In Your presence is **fullness** of joy; in Your right hand there are **pleasures forever**"* (Psa. 16:11). Many things in this world give us joy, our children/grandchildren, our faithful dog, a new car (for a few miles), good friends, and more. But ponder the word fullness, and then consider pleasures forever. Think how you feel when you experience joy in earthly things that will all be done away with. Now try to grasp that feeling never leaving you. I'd say that's a pretty good start to what Easter means.

The next thing Easter provides is hope. As I look around society, the common denominator of misery, unrest, selfishness that abounds is lack of hope. We have hoped in technology. It has dumbed us down to the point of not being able to carry on a reasonable conversation. We have hoped in government. I don't have to tell you how that worked out. We have hoped in riches. Fleeting. Gone.

Easter *fills* us with hope; hope for the future, hope for eternity. We know that this world will not improve until a complete reboot happens. Easter shows us it *will* happen because Jesus is alive. The Bible puts it into perspective: "*If we have hoped in Christ in **this life only**, we are of all men most to be pitied*" (I Cor. 15:19). But we have hope because Jesus is alive and made us a promise.

So what's the rest of the story? God is generous with His children. He wants us joyful. He wants us hopeful. He wants to give us good things. Why is there so much misery and desperation then? Read the qualifier at the end of our opening verse: "*to those who walk uprightly.*" Many of us are not willing to forego the pleasures of sin, which seem so fulfilling, so right because "everybody's doing it." First of all, everybody's NOT doing it. Secondly, we must live by standards, even in a Godless society, there must be commonly accepted rules, or you have anarchy and total chaos. Nobody is safe.

God's rules are not meant to restrict our fun. If you look closely at what the world deems fun, you'll see how shallow it is. It has no lasting value and must continually be tweaked to receive the same "pleasure" as yesterday (e.g. drugs). When the Holy Spirit is living is us, we have all the fruits—love, joy, peace, patience, kindness, goodness, self-control—available all the time. Doesn't that sound better than the misery of doing life the world's way? Easter is coming. Don't miss the significance that can be yours because Jesus is alive.

February 22, 2022

Aim at Nothing...

You're sure to hit it every time. Why do they call it target *practice?* Why do police, military, and Olympic biathletes spend **so much time** honing their shooting skills? So they can hit their target *every time.* Another word that belongs in this discussion is *goals.* It's been said that if you don't know where you're going, any road will lead you there.

As believers in Jesus Christ, we're to have goals too. Paul wrote to the Corinthian church, *"Whether, then, you eat or drink or whatever you do, do **ALL** to the glory of God* (I Cor. 10:31, emphasis added). The goal? God's glory. In his writings to the Roman church, Paul said, *"Do not be conformed to this world, but be transformed by the renewing of your mind, **so that** you may prove what the will of God is..."* (Rom. 12:2). The goal? Prove the will of God. And one more. In Matthew's gospel, Jesus says, *"**Seek first** the kingdom of God and His righteousness and all these things will be added to you"* (Matt. 6:33). The goal? Appropriation of God's righteousness into our life.

Do you see the common thread in these verses? They're orders from our commanding officer. For those of us who have served in the military, we know that if you don't follow orders, there are consequences (usually bad). That's true in the spiritual realm too. If you're saved and living in (habitual) sin, God won't necessarily punish you physically, at least not immediately, though there are examples in Scripture of it happening. But you will lose your joy, your closeness with your Father, fellowship with other pilgrims, and eternal rewards (not salvation).

Why is it so hard for some of us to set and keep goals? I can think of some reasons in my own life. Sometimes I focus on the "now" and not the endgame. Discipline is hard, sometimes boring. I'm lazy. I easily get distracted by shiny objects or "fun" things. Whatever the reason or excuse—I'm sure you have your own list—the bottom line is if I'm aiming at nothing, the result of not setting goals is the same as never hitting my target. Is that what God asks of us? Is that doing our very best as a loving response for who He is and all He's done and continues to do, for us?

We are to walk by faith. The Bible says, *"without faith it is impossible to please Him, for he who comes to God must believe that He is and that He is a rewarder of those who **seek** Him* ("seek" is an action verb) (Heb.11:6). Does goal setting please God? It depends. Does attainment of the goal fit into the "all" referenced above? God is not against us having things, losing weight, what we watch on TV, who we hang out with…as long as these things don't become idols and pull us away from our "doing all" and "seeking first". God's glory has to be our ultimate goal in life. Everything else will burn up.

You may think you've squandered your life. You may have guilt from bad decisions. It's not too late to start down a new path; one filled with blessings, joy, a future beyond comprehension. But you have to start. Take a first step. Call someone who is hurting. Look around with eyes tuned to needs—and meet one of them. A habit can be formed by doing something consistently for 30 days. Think about just the three goals above (2nd para.) and start by focusing on even one of them. Before you know it, you'll be less self-centered; you will experience joy from thinking about another person and, without hope of gain, you invested yourself in someone who had a need. You may think it a small thing. But if your motive is right, God knows it and records the act in His book of rewards.

Keep it up. Forget the shiny objects to the side of the road. Look straight ahead. Focus only on the big picture, the endgame, eternity. Will what you're offering to God survive the fire? Or will it be burned up? *"Now if any man builds on the foundation with gold, silver, precious stones, wood, hay, straw, each man's work will become evident; for the day will show it because it is to be revealed with fire, and the fire itself will test the quality of each man's work. If any man's work which he has built on it remains, he will receive a reward. If any man's work is burned up, he will suffer loss; but he himself will be saved, yet so as through fire"* (1 Cor. 3:12-15).

What are you aiming for today? We can always aim higher. So what if we miss? Review your life goals. Are they ones that will result in rewards or ashes? Are you still breathing? It's not too late. God loves to reward those who seek Him. Do it today. I'll hold.

February 25, 2022

Fear? Not!

Good story tellers save the dramatic revelation until the end hoping you are caught up in the clues to stay the distance. Today's good news fairly shouts off the page and hopefully, the application of it will be well worth the anticipation. We live in a society all but dominated by fear...of all kinds of things, people, and the future. The psalmist writes, *"In God, whose word I praise, In God I have put my trust; I shall not be afraid. What can mere man do to me?"* (Ps. 56:4).

I've taken a little liberty with the title of this message using some younger-generation vernacular. Over 200 times in Scripture we are told some variation of "fear not". Why do you think that is? A few times it was because an awesome, probably terrifying being—an angel (see Luke 1:12)—was sent to communicate a message to one or a group. Sometimes it was because God was about to lead His people through dangerous territory or into war.

Mostly it is because God is our all-powerful Father who can and does protect His children. In Hebrews 13:5 He says that He will **never** desert us or forsake us. Desert is a strong word implying even in the scariest situations, He won't abandon us. We know God *cannot* lie (Tit. 1:2). If this verse isn't enough, allow two more. The psalmist writes, *"cast your burden upon the Lord and He will **sustain** you. He will **never** allow the righteous to be shaken"* (Ps.55:22). And again from the Psalms, *"For he* [who fears the Lord] *will **never** be shaken; the righteous will be remembered **forever**"* (Ps. 112:6).

Never and forever. Great reminders of God's power and presence. I'm sure most of us know the 23rd psalm that starts out, *"The Lord is my shepherd."* But have you ever considered one of the most comforting promises in verse four? *"Even though I walk through the valley of the shadow of death,* (here it is) *I **fear no evil**, for You are with me."* There was a period in Israel's history when they were surrounded by 10 plagues that God brought upon the Egyptians. How many of those 10 plagues affected God's people? You can read the specifics in Exodus 9:6, 9:26, 10:23, 11:7, 12:3. Exactly zero.

For two years, our government leaders have bombarded us using fear tactics to control and compel compliance. They have blocked true science, put forth silly mask and distance requirements (which didn't seem to apply to BLM and ANTIFA) that have been proven ineffective. We've been pummeled day after day with death statistics. And when the political heat is becoming too much for them (they fear the mid-terms), they simply "change the science." How convenient. And all to what end? Their thirst for power, greed, and control. If you think it hasn't been effective, ask yourself why do you see lone drivers with windows rolled up wearing masks? Hmmm.

The Bible warned us against these men: "*In the last days difficult times will come. For men will be lovers of self, lovers of money, arrogant...irreconcilable...without self-control...haters of good, treacherous...avoid such men as these*" (2 Tim. 3:1-5). We have been in the last days since Christ was on earth. But is this the last of the last? I don't know. Neither does anyone else but God. Does it matter? Each of us has an expiration date, assigned by God before we were born (Ps. 139:16). Our job on earth is to obey the verse we talked about Tuesday (Aim at Nothing): "*do all to the glory of God.*"

Fear does not promote God's glory. Fear binds us, defeats us, keeps us on the bench out of the game. If you are afraid...of anything, ask yourself is the object of your fear something beyond God's ability to protect you? Is COVID? Is losing your job. Is the death of a loved one? Life happens. And it's ALL under God's sovereign control. Think about today's promises of God **never** leaving you, of "the righteous" **never** being shaken. Memorize these verses so the next time the tempter whispers in your ear "be afraid, be very afraid" you can combat him with the same weapon Jesus used in His 40 days in the desert...the Word of God.

The qualifier in this is that the verses only apply to "the righteous," those of us who have given our lives to Jesus Christ and who don't fear the future because we have a great expectation of Jesus' return to bring us to heaven to be with Him forever. If you don't have that confidence, check out our Appendix, *Steps to Salvation* in the back of this book. As a closing thought, ponder this verse, ask where I fall on the continuum: "*There is no fear in love; but perfect love casts out fear...*" (1 Jn. 4:18).

February 28, 2022

F.O.M.O.*

There is an event on the horizon that has been planned since before time began. To some reading this it will sound like science fiction, but I promise you every word is true. This event will happen. Can we schedule our lives around it? No, but we can and must be prepared. Nobody knows exactly the day or hour. All we know is…IT WILL come and it's the **one event** in your life, you don't want to miss. How can I be so sure? Because the God who created the universe said it, and He **cannot** lie (Tit. 1:2). I'm talking about The Rapture, a moment in time when Jesus calls His family from this earth to begin eternity with Him, to join Him in "the marriage supper of the Lamb" (Rev. 19:9). Prophetically speaking, there is nothing else that must happen before the Rapture. As a "pretrib Rapture believer" I believe this happens *before* the seven years of tribulation.

The second event is the time, seven years later, when Jesus physically returns to earth to judge all who haven't given their lives to Him in faith. It's called "the Day of the Lord" and it comes in two parts. I believe the first happens seven years after the *tribulation* starts. Judgment usually implies punishment. And in this case, it's severe and eternal. The second part of "The Day of The Lord" comes 1,000 years later, after the Millennial Kingdom of Christ on earth. This is the "Great White Throne Judgment" (Rev. 20:7,11).

"When you hear of wars and rumors of wars, do not be frightened; those things must take place; but that is not yet the end. For nation will rise up against nation, and kingdom against kingdom, there will be earthquakes in various places; there will also be famines. These things are merely the beginning of birth pangs" (Mark 13:7,8). Mankind has always had wars. Our nature of greed, self-centeredness, and lust for power has always spawned conflict between men and nations. And we've had famine and earthquakes throughout the earth.

Despite all this, God still loves His people and has always given warnings and wake-up calls before He acts. The Bible is our only survival guide to this devastating event. We've actually had over two millennia of warnings. Sadly, most people ignore these warnings. That's why Jesus said, *"Enter through the narrow gate; for the **gate is wide*** *and the way is broad that leads to destruction, and there are many who enter through it. For the gate is small and the way is narrow that leads to life, and there are few who find it"* (Matt. 7:13,14). Broad vs. narrow; wide vs. small; many vs. few. Not an encouraging picture of the end…unless you know Jesus as your Savior.

There's a reason "many" are on the wrong road. They've heard the warnings, they may even belong to a church, and God put it into their hearts to know Him, but they suppress the truth (Rom. 1:18,19). The "narrow" way is demanding, sacrificial, requires obedience to a holy God. The Bible says, *"This is the judgment, that the Light has come into the world, and men loved the darkness rather than the Light, for their deeds were evil"* (John 3:19). When your deeds are evil, you don't want accountability or anything that sheds light in your dark place.

You may have FOMO when it comes to social events with your friends and missing these may cause anxiety, jealousy, thoughts of revenge. But these are all temporary symptoms of a deeper need, the need to be loved and accepted as you are, without behavior modifications, to please a fickle crowd. There's only one place to find that unconditional love and acceptance, in a relationship with Jesus Christ. Jesus said, *"…the one who comes to Me I will certainly not cast out"* (John 6:37b). Have you come to Jesus and experienced His love and forgiveness? If so, thank Him that your future is secure. If not, FOMO associated with The Rapture should drive you to *"…seek Me [Jesus] with all your heart"* (Jer. 29:13) and *"Seek the Lord while He may be found"* (Isa. 55:6).

In our Appendix, *"Steps to Salvation"*, you'll find a detailed description of what God thinks of your condition apart from Him as well as Scripture that clearly states your predicament and how to deal with it. Most importantly, you'll erase FOMO linked to The Rapture and you'll know that you won't miss it, because you're a new creature in Christ (2 Cor. 5:17).

*(Fear Of Missing Out)

March 7, 2022

Weary, Wary, or Worry?

Today's title can cause us to pause and reflect on what's going on in the world and the effect it's had on us. We are **weary** of all the conflicting "science" pushing a COVID agenda of social distancing, ineffective mask mandates and unintended consequences, e.g. business closings. I'm being kind calling them "unintended." It has made us **wary** of anything coming out of the CDC or the White House, and it makes us **worry** about our future. It has shaken our trust and confidence in our leadership, be it political or "scientific." What should our response be?

There is an answer. Jesus told the crowds, *"Come to Me all who are weary and heavy laden, and I will give you rest" (Matt.11:28).* What did the crowds have to be weary from? Roman (read: government) oppression, capricious taxes, onerous regulations. You know, the same things we see in America today. How do we get rest from our weariness?

The first thing to remember is that nothing sneaks up on God. He is the undisputed ruler of the universe; He does whatever He pleases (Ps. 115:3). With that knowledge, we can be confident that Biden, Putin, and Xi Jinping are all doing exactly what God wants them to do. Secondly, what is happening around the world in every place, was planned before the first grain of sand appeared on earth (Gen. 1:9); it is not something that just showed up and God had to figure out how to deal with it. The end of life in time was planned then too.

Have you ever been to a movie and groaned when "The End" appeared on screen because you wanted more movie? There will be groaning and weeping and gnashing of teeth when God calls "the end"…except for those of us who know Jesus Christ as our Savior. We will be ecstatic with shouts of joy at our homecoming.

The other two Ws often creep in when our weariness leaves us down, depressed about the future, and doubting that God really knows what's going on. We become wary (cautious, guarded, untrusting) of everybody and everything. We worry (become anxious, fearful) about what will happen to the world and me specifically. If you find yourself in this quagmire, take a minute to reboot your relationship with God. Remember His promises. Here are a few:

*"Bless the Lord, O my soul, and forget none of His benefits; who **pardons all your iniquities**"* (Ps. 103:2).

*"I will **never desert you** nor will I ever forsake you"* (Heb. 13:5).

*"Vengeance is mine, **I will repay**, says the Lord"* (Rom. 12:19).

*"I go to prepare a place for you. If I go and prepare a place for you, **I will come again** and receive you to Myself, that where I am you may be also"* (John 14: 2,3).

…and there are so many more, all of which are available to each of us in our relationship with Jesus. Don't let what you read in the news or see on the TV be what you base your contentment, your peace, your hope on. All you need is Jesus and His word.

For encouragement, I suggest reading through the Psalms. Psalm 1 is a great place to start; only six verses but so powerful and encouraging for the family of God. We don't have to live with weariness about the present, wariness of people and circumstances, or worry about our tomorrows. Christ overcame all that at the cross. Let Him be the provider, the protector, and the peace that passes all understanding. He wants to. He's ready and willing to. **He's** just **waiting for us** to come to Him in humility and faith. What are *we* waiting for?

March 8, 2022

Crush or Edify

Words have meanings. Often it requires context because the same word can mean more than one thing, especially after modern slang has its go at it. Consider the word "bad." In my younger days, bad was what you called something you really liked. Confusing? Yes. Unmanageable? No. The Bible has a lot to say about the words that come out of our mouths. Our tongue is said to be "a fire" (Jas. 3:6). From our mouths come both blessing and cursing (Jas. 3:10). Paul cautions us about releasing "unwholesome words" (Eph. 4:29). Jesus said, "...*the mouth speaks out of that which fills the heart*" (Matt. 12:34b).

The full picture of the above verse from Ephesians 4:29 says, "*Let no unwholesome word proceed from your mouth, but only such a word as is good for edification according to the need of the moment, so that it will give grace to those who hear.*" When you look at these verses side by side you can see that our mouths and tongues are powerful for edification, comfort, encouragement, praise and more. But they can also be like the viper with poison that can crush in its vitriol, bitterness, hatred (Ps. 140:3).

I remember a little ditty from elementary school days when unkind names were hurled, "Sticks and stones will break my bones, but names will never hurt me." That's pure hogwash. Names called in anger, meanness, superiority can crush our spirits; they can have devastating consequences years into our futures.

Considering the context of words spoken, James asks the question, "*Does a fountain send out from the same opening both fresh and bitter water?*" (Jas.3:11). It's rhetoric. The answer is obviously no. But Jesus' words (para. 1) convict us of this very thing. Why? How is it possible to bless and curse from the same mouth? The answer is easy. The correction, not so much. The simple answer is we still sin. Our hearts are not as pure as we'd like to think, not as pure as we'd like others to think. And we have an enemy who delights in pushing just the right button to enable the flow.

So what's the solution? The first step is to humbly recognize we have this problem. Next, we must *want to change*. Until that happens, no amount of Bible reading, verse memorizing, or counseling will change the output. Unless we realize that our unkind, angry, hurtful words are sins that nailed Jesus to the cross, we will continue pounding the nails. But don't lose heart. Our walk of faith is based on the fact that *all* our sins were forgiven at the cross; past, present, and future. Go to God in prayer, confess that your heart isn't filled with "the right stuff."

Self-examination is a good next step. Ask yourself why you feel the need to put others down. Are you struggling with feelings of insecurity? Striking out at others may make us feel good for a moment, but it doesn't deal with the underlying issue. Ask, "Is my confidence in the flesh?" The answer is likely to be yes. As believers in Jesus Christ, our worth is not based on anything we do. We are valuable because God said we are, and Jesus gave His life to prove it. He loves us in spite of our warts. When we get our arms around that truth, it'll be easier to obey the command, "*...regard one another as more important than yourselves*" (Phil. 2:3b). Look at that verse again. It doesn't say others ARE more important. But if we consider them in that way, then the things coming out of our mouth will edify (enlighten, inspire) our hearers.

Today, there is so much of the other kind of speech everywhere we turn. Very little in the media or public arena edifies anybody. God's people are called to be different. Let's start in our own home and commit to only speaking words that edify our spouse, our children, and anybody else who passes our doorway. Maybe it'll catch on.

March 17, 2022

Murder or Love?

It is reported that on April 10, 2019, Irwin Jacobs, a very wealthy Minnesota businessman, took the life of Alexandra, his wife of 57 years, whom he adored, because she was suffering from dementia and had been wheelchair bound for the past year. He then turned the gun on himself and ended his own life. This is a tragic story on many levels. But that's not the point of this post. The question is, was it murder or love that prompted the act? There's no debate, Irwin pulled the trigger and unlawfully ended his wife's life. And that's the first part of the definition of murder. But the second part says, "especially with malice aforethought," clearly not part of Irwin's thinking.

Over 2,000 years ago, there was another death about which we could ask the same question: Was it murder or love? To be sure, the Jewish crowd killed Jesus in spite of having no legitimate charge, no evidence of wrongdoing against Him. And it certainly wasn't *their* love motivating the act, but a terrible hatred spawned by their rebellion. But here's the good news for us. It *was* love that orchestrated the hearts of those who carried it out. God's love for mankind. Love for you personally and me personally. Isaiah 53:10 says, *"But the Lord [God] was pleased to crush Him [Jesus]."* The writer of Hebrews tells us, *"Jesus…who for the joy set before Him endured the cross"* (Heb. 12:2). There's no greater description of love than these two verses.

What does that have to do with the society we live in? In a book written by A.W. Tozer (1897-1963) and published in 1961, *The Knowledge of The Holy*, Tozer writes, "The Church has surrendered her once lofty concept of God and has substituted for it one so low, so ignoble, as to be utterly unworthy of thinking, worshiping men. This she has done not deliberately, but little by little and without her knowledge; and her very unawareness only makes her situation all the more tragic." The past six decades have only exacerbated the problem and underscored the Church's failure to recognize the slippery slope of idolatry: the worship of anything but the one true God, including gods of your own thoughts and imaginations.

The greatest tragedy in this is that The Bible presents God in His splendor and majesty in a way any seeker can understand. But the

Church has largely diluted the message of God's holiness so that the God presented is nowhere near the God who is. Jesus wouldn't have said, *"Let the children alone and do not hinder them from coming to Me, for the kingdom of God belongs to such as these"* (Matt. 19:14) if the message were not simple enough for children to grasp.

The idea I'm trying to convey is simply that the God of the Bible is the answer to ALL of society's ills. Are you in a dark place, alone, despondent, bullied, fearful of your future? The true God of the Bible knows your inner longings, your failures, your heartache and, most importantly, He has the power and authority to heal anything you can throw at Him. Murder/suicide is the final act of desperation by someone who has depended on his own resourcefulness, his own strength and gotten nowhere in the only things in life that matter. Sure, you might have money in the bank. You might have your name on buildings and be a big donor to charity. But if you haven't answered the question, "What did you do with my Son Jesus?" all your money and fame won't survive the fires of judgment.

The prophet Jeremiah is having a conversation with God, and he has recited all of what God has done from creation to deliverance from Egypt, then God speaks to Jeremiah, *"Behold, I am the Lord, the God of all flesh; is anything too difficult for Me? "* (Jer. 32:27). Again, Jesus was talking with His disciples, and they were astonished at his teaching about salvation, *"And looking at them Jesus said to them, 'With people this is impossible, but with God **all** things are possible'"* (Matt. 19:26). So, nothing you are dealing with surprises God or is beyond His ability to heal if you'll let Him. You can take this to the bank: God loves you in spite of your warts and He's made a way for you to spend eternity with Him. That way is called Jesus. Jesus said, *"I am the way and the truth and the life, no one comes to the Father but through Me"* (John 14:6).

If you aren't sure about what waits for you after you die, check out the Appendix, *Steps to Salvation*. There, you'll get a clear picture of your condition without Jesus in your life. No matter how bleak things seem to you, nothing is beyond God's power to erase your past and shower you with more love than you'll know what to do with.

April 14, 2022

Immediate or Imminent?

Tomorrow is Tax Day in America. Sunday is Easter. Both events may spawn anxiety, even fear. While we understand the potential fear of dealing with the IRS—even if your reporting is totally honest—there are a lot of folks that *should* fear what Easter represents, especially if they don't embrace the truth of the event celebrated. Chocolate Easter bunnies, colored eggs, marshmallow "peeps" are the farthest things from the truth of Easter.

At first glance, you may read today's title and think, "what's the difference?" Immediate is a relative term. It means "near to or related to the present." Imminent, on the other hand, means "ready to take place at any moment without any further actions or events." Most of us live in an "immediate" frame of mind. We want what we want when we want it. We've all experienced the boss or auto mechanic, or salesman say something like, "I'll get on it immediately." When we'll see results depends on their definition of immediate and who controls the priority.

Imminent doesn't depend on anything external happening; it's ready now and could happen any moment, without warning. Fortunately, we've had millennia filled with warnings. So many warnings without apparent consequences, have led to a ho-hum apathy that I'm sure is why they've gone unheeded. But consider the penultimate verse of the entire Bible: (Jesus speaking) "*Yes, I am coming quickly.*" Bring it down to your personal level. Will your death be immediate or imminent? We can't answer that because we don't control the events leading to it. But God does.

Easter is the last chapter of God's love story to His family (see *No Good Thing*). The celebration of Jesus' resurrection from the grave proved God's authority over death, paid the full price for our redemption from sin, and fills us with hope for an indescribable eternity with Him. But…

As I look around our world and see the evil that is rampant everywhere, both here at home and abroad, and consider the warnings the world has had about Jesus Christ's return for His church, the word imminent takes on more significance. When it happens (imminent), it will be "in the twinkling of an eye (I Cor. 15:52)" and the family of Christ will be gone from the earth. Those who are left on earth—everybody who hasn't believed in Jesus' death and resurrection as total payment for their sins—are now facing seven horrific years of God's wrath.

If you're reading this, it's not too late. You may already be experiencing the seven years of God's wrath toward Satan's hate-fueled rebellion, or you may be bouncing along oblivious to the downward spiral of society's rejection of Jesus. As long as you have breath, you can turn from your sin and humbly embrace the truth that Jesus died for your sins too, no matter how bad you think they are. Jesus said, "...*the one who comes to Me, I will certainly not cast out* (Jn.6:37). For a detailed look at your position in God's eyes, check out the Appendix, *Steps to Salvation*. The empty cross and empty tomb are the truth about Easter, a truth that is filled with God's love, wonder, and amazing, awesome future for anyone who comes on His terms. I'll look for you there.

May 16, 2022

My Rights

You can't turn on the news or pick up a newspaper without some-body whining about their rights. In my opinion, many are trying to get something they didn't earn and don't deserve. The Bible is clear about people like this: *"…if anyone is not willing to work, then he is not to eat, either"* (2 Thess.3:10). I'm not denying that life is unfair in many respects. But why should I blame you for bad choices I make and vice versa? Choices have consequences…good or bad. And in a perfect world, we'd all accept that premise. But the last perfect world was God's Garden before Adam and Eve fell for the Big Lie.

In the United States, we are a nation ruled by laws. We *do* have rights. You know the list: assembly, speech, carry arms, etc. The prob-lem isn't the absence of rights, but their interpretation and application. When we each exercise our rights and they conflict, where do we draw the line? Greed and selfishness are ugly motivators.

We do have rights that cannot be taken away or abridged by polit-ical whim. Topping the list is the right to be obedient. The Prophet Samuel said, *"Behold, to obey is better than sacrifice* (1 Sam.15:22). This is likely a departure from what you were expecting, but think about it. If we were obedient to God's laws—which supersede manmade laws—there would be no stealing, coveting, adultery, and seven more that cover everything from A to Z. There would be peace in our hearts and in the world. It's not a dream, it's a promise from our Father. Certainly not here on earth yet but coming soon.

The other rights can be classified as subpoints under the main ten. For example, the right to put others first, the right to forgive others, the right to serve others, and many, many more. You might think I live in Mister Rogers' Neighborhood. I don't and I'm not trying to portray myself as having a perfect score in this area. But you and I have a conscience that innately sounds the alarm when we violate God's laws. That is, if we haven't disregarded it so often that it sounds more like a mourning dove than a 5-alarm fire engine.

What would that look like if everybody operated under these pa-rameters? It would be like a worldwide Garden of Eden…perfect. I'm trying to paint a picture of the coming appearance of Jesus Christ's millennial kingdom here on earth where all these things will be the norm not the exception. You don't want to miss it. But only those who are on the invited list will be welcomed. Have you received your invitation yet?

Invitations are easier to get than you think. They're free and available to everyone. There is only one requirement, that you come empty-handed. Advanced education won't get you in. Good deeds won't. Massive bank accounts won't. Any guilt over your sin will disqualify you. But there's good news. Your sin was paid for when Jesus died on a cross some 2,000 years ago. Your part is so simple many miss it and thereby won't get their name on the guest list. In humility, you must a.) recognize that you *are* a sinner and that left on your own you could never pay the price to erase your sin; b.) believe what the Bible says about sin (*"The wages of sin is death, but the free gift of God is eternal life in Christ Jesus our Lord"* [Rom. 6:23]); c.) believe what the Bible says, (*"If you confess with your mouth Jesus as Lord, and believe in your heart that God raised Him from the dead, **you will be saved**"* [Rom. 10:9 emphasis added]).

If you're thinking that this sounds too good to be true, you're not alone. Many think this and choose not to believe the simple truth from a God who *cannot lie* (Tit. 1:2). For a more detailed description of what God thinks about you personally, visit the Appendix, *Steps To Salvation* in the back of this book.

For you who have your invitation already, there's surely someone in your sphere of influence who is not yet on Jesus' guest list. Time is running out and tomorrow is not guaranteed to anyone. Pray that God would show you who needs to hear this good news and that He would empower you to open your mouth and share and keep sharing until you no longer have breath. See y'all at the feast.

May 17, 2022

No Shortages

Who'd ever thunk? Baby formula. Toilet paper. Job applicants. Shortages. And all blamed on COVID. Aren't you thankful that our God is not constrained by supply chain problems or pandemics?

The Bible tells us, *"And my God will supply all your needs according to His riches in glory in Christ Jesus"* (Phil. 4:19). Jesus also said, *"Do not worry then, saying 'What will we eat?' or What will we drink?' or 'What will we wear for clothing?'...your heavenly Father knows that you need all these things. But seek **first** His kingdom and His righteousness, and all these things will be added to you"* (Matt. 6:31-33). Did you notice the commonality of these verses? There are two. The first is the little word 'all'. The second is a condition we must meet to qualify. In the first example we must be 'in Christ Jesus'. In the second, we have to have our priorities right.

When God says 'all' He means all. His supply of mercy, grace, love, forgiveness is only limited by our lack of asking and lack of faith. The Apostle James puts it this way, *"But if any of you lacks wisdom, let him ask of God, who gives to all generously and without reproach, and it will be given to him. But he must ask in faith... You do not have because you do not ask. You ask and do not receive, because you ask with wrong motives, so that you may spend it on your pleasures"* (Jas. 1:5; 4:2).Know this: *God is able to do far more abundantly beyond all that we ask or think* (Eph. 3:20). Don't limit Him working in your life by not doing things His way.

What does it mean to be 'in Christ Jesus'? It means that we have put our faith (belief) and trust (for our eternal future) in Jesus' death and resurrection to eliminate our death penalty, deserved because of our sin and rebellion against God. It happens the very moment we turn from our self-rule and admit we have sinned and broken God's law and rightfully deserve death (*"the wages of sin is death"* Rom. 6:23). At that moment we become new creatures *"in Christ"* (*"If anyone is in Christ, he is a new creature; the old things passed away; behold, new things have come"* 2 Cor. 5:17).

What about our priorities? The second verse above tells us we must "seek first" God's kingdom and His righteousness. How do we do that? Spend time in your Bible on a daily basis (*"Establish Your Word to Your servant, as that which produces reverence for You"* Ps. 119:38), pray often about big and little things (*"pray without ceasing"* 1 Thess. 5:17), eliminate bad behavior (*"abstain from every form of evil"* 1 Thess. 5:22), and become involved in a Bible-believing church (*"let us consider how to stimulate one another to love and good deeds, not forsaking our own assembling together, as is the habit of some, but encouraging one another; and all the more as you see the day drawing near"* (Heb. 10:24, 25).

These are not magic formulas, nor are they genie-in-a-lamp wishes. They are rock-solid promises from the Creator of the universe that are there for the claiming by anyone who qualifies according to God's revealed plan. For a more detailed explanation than is given above, see Appendix, *Steps to Salvation* in the back of this book. But first, a word of caution.

Some have become discouraged because they thought they could manipulate God to do for them and give to them whatever they asked Him for. His promises are to supply all our **needs**, not all our **wants**. Growth in our relationship to God doesn't happen overnight. Our journey of faith is much like life; we start out as babies, unable to care for ourselves. We need milk, not steak, to grow. The simple truths of God's word are building blocks for a deeper relationship to Him. This is why we all need to spend time reading the Bible for ourselves. When you come to a verse or section you don't understand, pray for the Holy Spirit's guidance to open your eyes. That's why it's absolutely necessary to be part of a fellowship where together they study God's word.

This walk of faith is an exciting journey. We'll see God in His creation and praise Him for it. We'll see Him in answers to prayer that changes hearts and circumstances that couldn't change any other way and praise Him for it. He will become real in the pages of Scripture and the historic events written there will become sources of encouragement for our own walk. Don't wait to get started.

June 1, 2022

Woke is not Awake

Alarm clocks. The smell of frying bacon and brewing coffee. What does it take to wake you up? We're living in a time when many believe they are on the leading edge of societal evolution, championing the move into the future while leaving outdated and irrelevant thinking and ways behind; all the while, scoffing at anybody who isn't on the same bandwagon.

The sad truth, as Solomon put it around 900 BC, "*That which has been, is that which will be, and that which has been done, is that which will be done. So there is nothing new under the sun* (Eccl. 1:9)." The world had become so wicked only six chapters into Genesis, ("*Then the Lord saw that the wickedness of man was great on the earth, and that every intent of the thoughts of his heart was only evil continually* [Gen. 6:5]"), that God destroyed **everything** that had breath—people and animals—except for 8 people and the animals Noah took into the ark.

What is the purpose of alarms, of warning signs? Isn't it to change behavior, direction, or thinking and avoid consequences of continuing the same path? Sometimes we don't have a lot of time to think about the warning. For example, a sign that says "Bridge Out Ahead" may only give us a few hundred feet to decide what to do. A weather warning may only give a few hours or even minutes to react. And these are obvious. What about warnings that are not as near-term? Things like "do your homework" aren't always tied to the immediate future. But sooner or later there will be consequences.

Lest you think that God is unfair, the people of Noah's day had about a hundred years of Noah preaching righteousness while he built a 450 ft.-long ark. Listen to God's heart about the wicked, "*I take no pleasure in the death of the wicked, but rather that the wicked turn from his way and live* (Ezek. 33:11)". God always gives warnings before He pronounces and enacts judgment. In the following examples, the **warnings are to God's people**.

"*Do this, knowing the time, that it is already the hour for you to* **awake** *from sleep; for now salvation is nearer to us than when we believed. The night is almost gone, and the day is near. Therefore let* *us lay aside the deeds of darkness and put on the armor of light. Let us behave properly as in the day, not in carousing and drunkenness, not in sexual promiscuity and sensuality, not in strife and jealousy. But put on the Lord Jesus Christ, and make no provision for the flesh in regard to its lusts* (Rom. 13:11-14)".

*"...Therefore, if you do not **wake up**, I will come like a thief, and you will not know at what hour I will come to you* (Rev. 3:3)".

*"Thus says the Lord God, 'A **disaster, unique disaster**, behold it is coming! An end is coming; the end has come! It has awakened against you; behold it has come! Your doom has come to you* (Ezek. 7:5-7)".

The church in America and around the world has become anemic, weak, lazy. It has shelved the Word of God in favor of psychobabble, new-age, and "woke" philosophies claiming the Bible has no answers for "modern" man. That is a lie from the father of lies: Satan himself. First, the Bible is true cover to cover. It is the only book that accurately portrays both sides of God: His love, mercy, and grace as well as His righteous judgment and wrath. Second, while destruction is promised and surely coming, the Bible gives the ***ONLY WAY*** TO ESCAPE GOD'S WRATH: JESUS CHRIST (John 14:6). Escaping God's wrath is a by-product of the real reason you need to embrace Jesus. God's love, mercy and grace—all undeserved—is beyond our comprehension, but available to all who repent and turn from their sin.

The warnings have been clearly sounded for millennia. If we're not ready, we can't blame anybody but ourselves. Church, it's time to wake up. If your love for God and His word has dimmed, do whatever is necessary to fire it back up. The time is short. We won't get any more advance notice before Christ returns. Look around. Read the symptoms. We have become a godless society. Get excited about being in the presence of Jesus, the perfection of heaven and its joy, peace, lack of pain, sorrow, lying, hatred, divisiveness. We're going soon. Make sure that you know Jesus personally and you're not just sitting in a pew. Remember the story of the five wise and five foolish virgins. All were waiting for Jesus, but half didn't get in (Matt. 25:1-13). Hope to see you there.

August 1, 2022

God in the Furnace

The Christian experience is totally about faith. Faith in something seen is not faith. *"Now faith is the assurance of things hoped for, the conviction of things not seen."* Heb. 11:1 It's always in something we can't see…until we're already into it. Take the account of Shadrach, Meshach, and Abednego in Daniel 3. They got on the wrong side of King Nebuchadnezzar because they wouldn't bow to his golden idol. Their faith in the true God infuriated Neb (Dan. 3:13,19) and he turned up the heat, planning to burn the trio alive.

Not only did they refuse the king's order to bow down, but their faith emboldened them to "speak truth to power" to put it into today's vernacular. Their response disclosed how strong their faith was, *"…He will deliver us out of your hand, O king. **But even if He does not**, let it be known to you, O king, that **we are not going to serve your gods** or worship the golden image that you have set up."* (Dan. 3:17,18) They didn't try to negotiate with God or put Him in a box. They left the decision about their future entirely in His hands.

I wonder if, and hope that, I would have that kind of faith when faced with my own fiery furnace. The point of the story is this, there was no sign of anybody in the furnace when the three were bound and thrown into the fire. Immediately a fourth "man" was seen walking about with the other three, unbound and unharmed. God could have protected them without showing Himself and it still would have been a miraculous ending resulting in a change in the king. But He chose to honor and strengthen the faith of His servants by confirming His presence. Can you imagine their elation, their joy at realizing they were safe in the company of the creator of the universe?

The Israelites, led by Joshua, were on the move to the promised land. There was a small problem. The river Jordan at this time of year was overflowing its banks. (Jos. 3:15) Joshua was a man of strong faith and knew God wouldn't lead them in an impassable path. As in the account above, they couldn't see how they would cross but God had told Joshua that when the priests' feet hit the water, it would be cut off. They literally stepped out in faith and God stopped the water flow about 15 miles upstream and they crossed on dry ground. (Jos. 3:17)

What can we take away from these events? First, God has not and never will change. He's in the business of giving and growing our faith in Him. Because He's the same yesterday, today and forever, we can expect the same seemingly insurmountable trials, call them our own personal furnaces and rivers. Second, His deliverance will be in ways that bring glory to *Him*, not to us and our ingenuity or cleverness. Third, our faith is expanded to new depths of trust in the unseen and with each new trial, we anticipate God's solution. The result is that our testimony to God's involvement in His children's lives becomes a powerful witness that cannot be refuted by scoffers.

I hope you're experiencing God's protection and provision as we face uncertain times. It certainly seems like something new and different, from a historical perspective, is exploding all around us. The forces of evil are everywhere, even, maybe especially, in the church. We cannot expect to be kept *from* it all (*"it rains on the righteous and the unrighteous"*[Matt. 4:45]), but we can trust God to keep us *in* whatever He allows. Hear an encouraging promise for those of us who know Jesus as our Lord and Savior, *"The hand of our God is favorably disposed to all those who seek Him, but His power and His anger are against all those who forsake Him* [Ezra 8:22]" If you don't know Jesus, it's not too late. Check out the Appendix, *Steps to Salvation* at the back of this book. It's the only way to have eternal fire and flood insurance.

August 16, 2022

Start Small…but Start

A journey of any distance begins with the first step. If we're going to accomplish anything, go anywhere, we need to take that first step. And we have to know where we're going. You know, set a goal. Olympic athlete wannabes don't wake up one morning and decide they're going to try out for the games. Years of focus and discipline are required to even qualify to be considered. Goals, small at the outset and successfully achieved, are what encourage us to set bigger, more aggressive goals. It becomes a cycle: set a goal…reach it…expand it…repeat. This is true in every endeavor worth pursuing. Goal setting keeps us from floundering. Reminds me of a Chuck Berry song from 1965, "No Particular Place to Go."

The Christian life is like that too. We don't start out with a faith that is ready and willing to die for the cause of Christ. Consider the disciples. They had spent nearly three years personally involved with Jesus in the flesh. And yet every one of them deserted Him that night in the garden. No, God brings us along by designing trials specifically for us that are not beyond what we can handle, and He also provides the escape route (I Cor. 10:13).

You ever wonder why God allows trials in the lives of His children? I have. We find the answer in God's Word. Isaiah writes in 55:11 comparing God's word to planting seeds, *"So will My word be which goes forth from My mouth; it will not return to Me empty, without accomplishing what I desire, and without succeeding in the matter for which I sent it."* And Paul, from his imprisonment in Rome shackled to his guards, is encouraged to speak God's word boldly so that the whole praetorian guard has had the gospel preached and even some in Caesar's household had responded (Phil. 1:13, 4:22). God accomplishes *His* purposes through *our* trials. That's the God side of the answer. James gives us our side of the answer (1:3,4), *"…testing of your faith produces **endurance**…so that you may be **perfect** and **complete**, lacking in nothing."*

Let's assume that you want your faith to grow so you're able to stand against the powers, world forces of darkness and spiritual forces of wickedness in heavenly places (Eph. 6:12). How does it happen?

Relate it to a journey. It starts with a first step, then another and another. Consistently walking in obedience to the revealed will of God will prepare us for the trials God has designed. When we see God act on our behalf through our faith, we are strengthened for the next. Each trial we endure grows our trust that not only is God *able* to deliver us (remember Shadrach, Meshach, and Abednego [Daniel 3]) but that He *will* deliver us. And we can say with Job, *"though He slay me, I will hope in Him* Job 13:15)."

Wherever you are on *your* journey, there's always a next step. If you're just starting out, there are two things you must do. First, decide where you're going (heaven or hell), second, take the first step. If you want to go to heaven but don't have a map or think that heaven is for "good" people, you need to visit the Appendix, *Steps to Salvation* in the back of this book for directions. Maybe that'll be your first step. Then keep walking. Hope to see you on the other side.

September 10, 2022

Jewels or Junk?

"Now if any man builds on the foundation with gold, silver, precious stones, wood, hay, straw, each man's work will become evident; for the day will show it because it is to be revealed with fire and the fire itself will test the quality of each man's work" (I Cor. 3:13,14).

Life is filled with choices. Simple ones like what to eat, what to wear and more complex ones like who to marry, what career, where to live. Consequences follow our choices. Some good, some not so good. We can get through most of them, even the bad ones. But there is one choice that is literally between life and death…for everyone.

Over my career, I've built two new houses. Both were learning experiences, not really good or bad, but I probably won't do it again. First of all, I'm trying to downsize. My kids' kids are all adults and my wife and I are considering doing more traveling. I'd love to have a "lock and leave" condo. The question is where? Second, with the cost and shortage of materials today, I'm sure I would have to double up on my blood pressure meds.

There is an obvious similarity between the building materials for a house and the two types of building materials mentioned in our verse. Stone and brick can withstand more than wood and hay when it comes to fires. It's just a matter of definition, because the materials described in today's verse are representative of the good we do *after* we have come to know Jesus Christ as our Lord and Savior. Before that event, all of our *"righteous deeds are like a filthy garment"* (Isa. 64:6). The Israelites were a stubborn, sometimes obnoxious bunch, that had a hard time following God's law. This comment was part of a prayer of confession that Isaiah was making to God on their behalf.

Before you think I'm promoting good deeds as a way to earn our way into heaven, I'm not. The Bible is **very** clear on that matter: *"For by **grace** you have been saved **through faith**; and that **not of yourselves**, it is the gift of God; **not as a result of works**, so that no one may boast"* (Eph. 2:8,9). In our verse above, Paul is writing to **the church** in Corinth warning them that even though they may be saved, righteous living, pure hearts, keeping short sin accounts with God through repentance and forgiveness, is the "fire insurance" for rewards.

Dr Erwin Lutzer has a provocative little book, *Your Eternal Reward,* in which he differentiates between salvation, which cannot be lost, and rewards promised by Jesus (see Rev. 22:12), which *can be lost.*

I write this by way of encouragement for those of us who know Jesus, and by way of warning to those who don't. As I said above, choices have consequences. If you are saved, my question is simply, "How are you doing in your "gold and jewel" gathering (good deeds done to honor God)? Remember what Jesus said, "*Do not store up for yourselves treasures on earth, where moth and rest destroy, and where thieves break in and steal. But **store up for yourselves treasures in heaven**...*" (Matt. 6:19). And Paul, again writing to the church at Corinth, "*...we must **all** appear before the judgment seat of Christ**, so that** each one **may be recompensed** for his deeds **in the body**, according to what he has done, whether good or bad*" (2 Cor. 5:10). This reminder is for **the church**. Nobody is "in the body" unless they are saved.

If you have yet to meet Jesus personally, take a few minutes and visit the Appendix, *Steps to Salvation* in the back of this book. There is nothing you have done or continue to do that will keep you from a relationship to God through Jesus. Reread the Ephesians verse above. It's A GIFT from the God who created you, who loves you and wants to spend eternity with you. You can't even begin to imagine the good and perfection that awaits you in heaven. Jesus said, "*...the one who comes to Me, I will certainly not cast out*" (John 6:37). I look forward to meeting you there.

October 31, 2022

No Good Thing...

With this title, there are a lot of ways the post could go. It could be a summary of my life's work. It could be a description of our current political and world climate. Or it could be what it is: the opening of a great promise from Psalms. The rest of the verse says, *"does God withhold from those who walk uprightly* (Ps. 84:11b)." Think about that. No...good...thing. Have you ever wanted anything that wasn't a good thing? I can think of a few. But enough about me.

Don't you love that the Bible is filled with amazing promises that are available to all? If this is true, and it is, why do we not get the answers to prayer we want? Spoiler alert, most of God's promises come with a condition. In fact, they're more like a contract with each side having an obligation. It's like an "if-then" clause in software. IF the user does a certain action, THEN a programmed response happens...every time.

In our verse today, our obligation is to walk uprightly. What does that mean? It means we're to *"come out from their midst and be separate, says the Lord. And do not touch what is unclean* (2 Cor. 6:17)." Today's church, especially in America, has gotten so far away from God's standard of holiness, that it's a wonder God answers any of our prayers. Consider just one example. "He made them male and female" (people and animals). There are 19 references to male and female just in the book of Genesis. Anything else is a lie from Satan. All the gender-identification nonsense, the excuses that blame God for "making me this way," and parental look-the-other-way because Johnny thinks he's Jenny, are nothing more than the latest version of false religion. And they will reap the fruit of their rejection of the truth. *"For the wrath of God is revealed from heaven against all ungodliness and unrighteousness of men who suppress the truth in unrighteousness, ...so that they are without excuse (Rom. 1:18-20).*

The church is not immune from this indictment. Many churches (not all praise God, but many) have embraced this aberrant, deviant, "big-tent" philosophy of inclusion, trying to justify it by cloaking it in God's love. Know this: When eternity is at stake, the most loving thing we can do is tell the truth. The mumbo-jumbo that the world tries to peddle as truth is nothing more than lies from hell, that non-believers, who don't have the Holy Spirit's discernment, swallow hook, line, and sinker and regurgitate as though anybody who didn't embrace this "enlightenment" was an idiot.

Since today is Halloween, permit one more example. What is Halloween anyway? It began in early practices by superstitious Celtic pagans of building huge bonfires and sacrificing animals and crops to appease Celtic deities. They believed that on this day the lines between living and dead were blurred. At these festivals, they wore "costumes" of animal heads and skins and attempted to tell each other's future. After a list including witchcraft, sorcery, divination, mediums and spiritists, (all these are forbidden in Scripture) Deut. 18:14 says, *"the Lord your God has not allowed you to do so."* And another to the same issue, *"He did much evil in the sight of the Lord* (2 Chron. 33:6). So it's clear what God thinks about this demonic activity promoted by the forces of darkness.

Like everything in our world, if it isn't from God, it starts out innocuous then over time gathers speed and includes followers who aren't up to date in knowing their Bible. One reason it won't ever go away is it has become a huge money-making commercial activity. Over one-fourth of all candy sold annually is for Halloween. Over $6 billion is spent on Halloween, second only to Christmas spending. Consider the similarity. The creation of Santa Claus is the hook that reels in millions of kids, greedy for the shiny things on display. Parents cannot say no to the excessive media blitz for commercialism both for Christmas and Halloween. Where is the church in speaking out about this?

But I digress. IF we walk uprightly, which includes saying no to worldly things which draw us away from God, THEN we will be the recipients of *good things* from God. How do I know? The Bible tells me so.

If you're on the fence, I invite you to visit the Appendix, *Steps to Salvation* in the back of this book for a clear picture of how God views you and the wonder and beauty that await all of us who trust Jesus Christ for the righteousness required to enter heaven.

November 25, 2022

God's Will

Anybody ever ask you, "How do I know God's will?" There are two possibilities why they would ask. The first is that they don't spend time in God's word and haven't been exposed to it. I was reading in Zechariah this morning and came across a section in chapter 8 that jumped off the page because it couldn't have been plainer. God speaking through Zechariah, "**These are the things you should do**: speak the truth...judge with truth...do not devise evil in your heart...do not love perjury, all these are **what I hate**." Did you notice three of the four things deals with the truth: telling it, judging with it, hating its antithesis? Honesty, integrity, purity of thought and action are high on God's list of *His* will, *our* what-to-dos.

Proverbs 6:16-19 has a list of seven things the Lord hates, among them two of the seven deal with lying. Just the word lying, appears over 65 times in the Bible. Regardless of where you might be in your reading, if you're spending any time at all, you'll likely come across something about lying. So the excuse might go like this: "I just have a hard time understanding what I'm reading." That could be true for several reasons. You might be using ye olde translation, aka King James. Or you could be a new Christian and have to look up the location of books in the index. Or you could be guilty of stretching the truth because you're lukewarm or lazy, or don't have reverence for God (Ps.119:38). Which brings us to the second reason.

You have read His word but don't think the "restrictive" standards apply to you as much as to "Bob." You need the section on the log and the speck (Matt. 7:3; Luke 6:41). You're looking for a verse like Jeremiah 29:11, often taken out of context, which says, *"For I know the plans I have for you," declares the Lord, "plans for prosperity and not disaster, to give you a future and a hope."* This verse is a promise to Israel when they are in the middle of a 70-year exile in Babylon. But many preachers use it as a "proof text" for their prosperity gospel...then they ask you to dig deep and send a donation. They are also guilty of violating today's topic. They are not "rightly handling the word of truth" (2 Tim. 2:15).

Lest you think I'm accusing others of purposely misleading for whatever reason, I'm just the messenger. You've heard the saying, "If the shoe fits…." The point is that God's word is clear about His commands. Every time you see one, make a note. That's part of God's will. What you do with it will determine whether you hear "Well done" or "Depart from me" when you see Jesus at the final judgment.

Here's a few just in the verses following verse 15 above: **flee** youthful lusts; **pursue** righteousness; **refuse** foolish and ignorant speculations; be **kind**, be **skillful** in teaching, be **patient** when wronged. These **six commands** appear in just three verses (22-24). Notice three are action words and three are attitudes. I call them the "do-attitudes" and the "be-attitudes" (see Matt.5:3-11). They are peppered throughout Scripture, if one only wants to see them for what they are: God's will.

It all starts in our heart/mind. We have to be honest seekers of God's will and have intention of obeying what we're shown. We're told in Rom. 12:2 not to be conformed to the world, but be transformed by renewing our minds. Why? **So that** you may **prove what the will of God is**. As an aside, look up how many times the phrase "so that" appears in Scripture. God **always** has purpose in what He says and does.

Let's go back to my original question. The next time you're in a conversation about knowing the will of God, remember this post, especially the parts about "skillful in teaching" and "be patient" because at that moment, you're the teacher. Not to dissuade or scare you into avoiding the issue, but to remind you that as teachers, we have a greater responsibility to teach the truth (James 3:1).

If you were hoping to find here the answers to which job to take, which house to buy, which…anything, don't try to run before you walk. But **if** you can honestly say you're doing these things above, **then** you're in the kind of relationship with God that allows you to do whatever you want because His Spirit will steer you toward choices that honor Him.

Glad you took the time to read this. May God grant you your heart's desire to know Him, love Him and serve Him better today than yesterday.

November 30, 2022

Scripture Sandwich

I'm always glad when my daily Bible reading brings me to Romans 8. I wrote about it two years ago in *Good News Monday.* I've probably been through it three or four times since. Today I had a new thought while reading. Isn't it great that God's word never gets stale? You've heard of "feeding on the word" and "bread of life." I know, Jesus said, "*I* am the bread of life." But John 1 tells us that Jesus *is* the word [of life]. It's not a stretch to equate word and bread.

Today I discovered a "sandwich" in Romans 8. One "slice of bread" is the first verse, "*Therefore there is now no condemnation for those who are in Christ Jesus.*" The other slice is the last three verses of the chapter, "*But in all these things we overwhelmingly conquer through Him who loved us. For I am convinced that neither death, nor life, nor angels, nor principalities, nor things present, nor things to come, nor powers, nor height, nor depth, nor any other created thing, will be able to separate us from the love of God which is in Christ Jesus our Lord.*"

What are "all these things" referred to in v.37? Between "no condemnation" and "overwhelmingly conquer" is a list of what Paul tells us we conquer. I'm just going to skim it because my purpose today is to try to get you excited about God's word in general…and do something about it.

There's a section about flesh vs. spirit and the war in that arena. Sufferings are prevalent throughout our life. You've heard the saying, "life is tough and then you die." There's more than a little truth in that. We are told that the sufferings of "this present time" v.18, "*are not worthy to be compared to the glory that is to be revealed to us.*" Though written 2,000 years ago, we too, in *this* present time, are suffering as a society when nothing enacted by Congress resembles a "Nation Under God." We are reminded that we "groan" waiting for heaven. But then the good stuff starts. "*God causes all things to work together for good to those who love God, to those who are called according to His purpose (v28).*" We are encouraged, "*If God is for us who is against us? (v31)*" And the best, Jesus himself is praying for us (v34).

Then (drum roll) Paul says, "but," which implies that whatever the struggles and suffering we've gone through or are going through now (listed above in 2nd para.), is nothing that has any lasting effect on our love relationship with God, our father. It would be like Pop Warner trying to take on the NFL.

Let's focus on the good stuff. Verse 28 doesn't say all things work together for good. It says God *causes* all things to work together for good. When we know God through Jesus Christ, He orchestrates all events for our good and His glory. This is one of many verses we should have in our arsenal to combat the lies of the devil. There's more. We *overwhelmingly* conquer. We don't just squeak by and sneak into heaven. It's a full-on victory celebration, not for us, but for Christ who won the battle on our behalf. We are part of the glorious feast because we have a personal invitation from Jesus, "*…the one who comes to me, I will certainly not cast out* (Jn. 6:37)." Once we're "in the family", verses 37-39 should give us comfort, confidence, and conviction to share the good news.

Whether you like a meat sandwich or PB&J, there's plenty in the Bible to choose from. Read Psalm 19:7-11 for a Bible-101 tutorial as to what Scripture has to offer. Just to highlight the key words from these verses: perfect, sure, right, pure, clean, true, more desirable than gold, warnings, great reward. I'll add one more from another Psalm (119:160): everlasting.

The world offers anything but perfect, pure, clean, true, or everlasting. And its packaging is enticing. If we're not read up in our time in the Bible, we'll likely fall prey to our flesh's desires and before we know it, things of God are a speck in our rear-view mirror. Fellow believers, time is short. Persevere in your walk. Another verse from Psalm 119 is the key. Verse 11 says, "*Your word I have treasured in my heart that I may not sin against You.*" Are you treasuring God's word today? Do you look forward to your time in it? Are you obeying what you read? Jesus said, "Heaven and earth will pass away but My words **will not pass away** (Matt. 24:35)." I encourage you to let go of anything that won't survive with you in your transition into the afterlife.

January 3, 2023

Victim or Victor

The year is gone. The time has come to put it in the rearview and move on. As we look ahead to 2023, we have a choice to make. We can accept the mantle of victim and wallow in self-pity and blame if we've experienced a not-what-we-hoped-for year. Or we can thumb our collective noses at the past 365 days and look forward with an attitude of I-faced-it-and-I'm-still-here victor mentality.

I know, with all that went on in 2022, it doesn't feel much like a victory celebration. Some of us faced serious loss, of health, money, jobs, loved ones. And those are clearly blows that can be devastating...if we let them by dwelling on them. Please don't misunderstand. I'm not downplaying the seriousness of any trial you've gone through. It was a tough year for many of us.

But for those of us who know Jesus Christ as our Savior and Lord, His promises are what we need to focus on. Here's just a sample: *"I will **never leave you** or forsake you"* (Heb. 13:5). *"In My Father's house are many rooms; **if that were not so, I would have told you**, because **I am going there to prepare a place for you**. And if I go and prepare a place for you, **I am coming again and will take you to Myself**, so that where I am, there you also will be"* (John 14:2-4). *"The Lord is **my** shepherd, I shall not want. **He** makes **me** lie down in green pastures; **He** leads **me** beside quiet waters. **He** restores **my** soul; **He** guides **me** in the paths of righteousness...even though I walk through the valley of the shadow of death, I fear no evil, for **You are with me**..."* (Ps. 23:1-4).

These three verses point to the *personal* relationship we have with Jesus Himself. Look at the highlighted words and imagine Jesus speaking directly to just you. There's one more verse I've chosen to wrap a bow on this thought: Romans 8:37-39, *"But in all these things we **overwhelmingly conquer through Him** who loved us. For I am convinced that neither* *death, nor life, nor angels, nor principalities, nor things pre-sent, nor things to come, nor powers, nor height, nor depth, **nor any other created thing**, **will be able to separate us from the love of God, which is in Christ Jesus our Lord.***"

The world, and specifically Satan, hates Jesus and by ex-tension, they hate us. They will do everything in their power, e.g. forced compliance with masks and vaccines, shuttering businesses, closing schools, to try to separate us from our com-mitment to Christ. When our time in God's word is anemic or rare, it's easy to buy into the hype of those "in charge" of our society and swallow their narrative. Their end is described in detail in Romans 1:18-32.

Psalm 33:18-19 should give us even more hope, "*Behold, the eye of the Lord is on those who fear Him, on those who hope for His lovingkindness, to deliver their soul from death and to keep them alive in famine.*"

What better message to begin the year than a reminder for those of us in Christ that WE ARE ON THE WINNING TEAM. Our future is secure, we have an advocate (Jesus) with God Himself on our behalf, and the trials we face on this earth are "*momentary, light affliction*" (2 Cor.4:17). It may not seem like momentary or light while we're in them and we may ask ques-tions such as "why me?" or "why now?" thinking God unfair. But remember that you are God's child and "*For those whom the Lord loves, he disciplines, and he scourges **every** son whom He receives*" (Heb. 12:6). "*We walk by faith, not by sight*" (2 Cor.5:7). *Everything* God does is for *our good* (Heb.12:10).

Paul adds another encouragement in Phil. 3:12-14, "*…but one thing I do: **forgetting what lies behind** and **reaching for-ward to what lies ahead**, I press on toward the goal for the prize of the upward call of God in Christ Jesus.*"

When we think about all we have waiting for us in heaven, all that God has done for us in Jesus to get us there, how can we not be thrilled and excited about the time being short before we are called home. New years can be a time of new beginnings, new thoughts, new habits. Has your fervor for service in the

King's army waned over the past months? Do you find your time in His word getting shorter each day? There are nearly a dozen verses from Jesus' own lips warning us to stay alert for the time is near. Hear one example directly from Jesus, *"Therefore be on the alert, for you do not know which day your Lord is coming."* (Matt. 24:42).

Paul talks about a goal, a prize, an upward call. What goals have we set for ourselves starting now? I don't like to call them resolutions, because once you mess up, your guilt whispers "I knew you couldn't do it." But with God-honoring goals, we don't have to be perfect. Remember the Lord's prayer, "Forgive us this day…" That's the good news of Jesus in a nutshell…forgiveness and new beginnings. But we have to start. Make a commitment in your heart or publicly that you will be more disciplined in your Bible time, more faithful in your prayer time, and more humble in your "me" time. If you do that, you'll find that your "me" time will be spent more in your Bible and prayer time. Wouldn't that be something?

The best thing to leave you with is this thought. You don't have to do it alone. God has given us the Holy Spirit and, *"when He, the Spirit of truth comes, He will guide you into all the truth; for He will not speak on His own, but whatever He hears, He will speak; and He will disclose to you what is to come"* (John 16:13).

Have a blessed new year trusting and serving the Lord Jesus.

January 13, 2023

Christ in the Crisis

What is a crisis? Where do they come from? Why me? Crises come in all shapes and sizes, from a bad haircut to the sudden death of a loved one. From the inane to heart-attack serious. Each person has their own definition of what constitutes a crisis for them. And we can't judge their rationale, their emotional maturity, stage in life, or anything that belies our attitude of superiority. We have no idea of circumstances leading up to someone else's crisis. We are not the measuring stick by which the legitimacy of their crisis is measured.

For those of us who live in America, many of the things we label "crisis" don't compare to most of the world whose crises regularly consist of lack of food, clothing, and shelter. Consider the people of Ukraine. I'm not saying their conditions prior to Russia's attack were ideal. But nobody deserves unprovoked bombings and killings like Putin has foisted on Ukraine.

"An emotionally significant event or radical change of status in a person's life" is how Webster's defines a crisis. Ukraine is a current example of a societal crisis. But there are also emotional crises, like fear, insecurity, loneliness and more. What can often be the result of letting these personal emotional crises go untreated? Is there a common denominator, a root cause manifesting itself in various symptoms?

I'm not a trained psychologist, psychiatrist, or counselor. But I am one who knows, loves, and trusts the word of God. In my experience, I've never found anything in God's word to be untrue. Permit just one example of "worldly" wisdom vs. God's word. The "professionals" tell us, "Don't spank." How's that working out? The Bible counsels, "*He who withholds [spanking] hates his son, but he who loves him disciplines him diligently* (Prov. 13:24)." In one to two generations (mine and my kids') we have gone from discipline practices of parenting that were common, to those that are nearly non-existent.

As a firm believer in God's word, I have lived a life of faith which has given me a "peace of God which surpasses all comprehension (Phil. 4:7)" and that has the ability to eliminate all fear. My wife of over 51 years and I have been through the fire a number of times. We have buried two children, been out of work almost three years from a motorcycle accident which wasn't my fault, been cheated out of a very large sum of money, and in spite of it all, we have not lost our faith in the God who said, "*For the Lord your God is a compassionate God; He will not abandon you nor destroy you,* (Deut. 4:31). Did we like the trials? No. Did it shake our trust in God? No. God *always* has purpose in everything He allows.

I believe that until the most important question in life is dealt with and answered, mankind will be bound by fear. The question? Where will you spend eternity? I've heard all the denials and excuses you can imagine. "There is nothing after you die." "I've led a good, moral life. I'm just going to take my chances." "I don't believe all the Bible stuff." "I'm not ready, I'll look into it sometime. Right now I've got things I want to accomplish."

The Bible has a word for people who have this type of response: "fool." Jesus told a parable about a rich man who had the attitude that he and his riches would go on for a long time, *"But God said to him, 'You fool! This very night your soul is required of you; and now who will own what you have prepared'?* (Luke 12:20). I have experienced this truth twice and believe me, it wakes you up to the brevity of life.

Above, I asked the question, "Is there a common denominator?" The answer is absolutely, yes. How can I say that? Aside from personal experience—which can be counterfeited by the enemy of our souls—the Bible has many examples of this truth. Consider Daniel protected from hungry lions (Dan. 6:7-24). Consider Shadrach, Meshach, and Abednego protected *in* a fiery furnace (Dan. 3). And there are many more. Some will say that these are fanciful tales, children's bedtime stories. That's sad. The first bridge you must cross to gain understanding is to accept that the Bible is true cover to cover. If you can't do that, there's no need to read any of it. How would you know what's true and what isn't?

Assuming you're still with me, the title of this is "Christ in the Crisis." He *is* with you in your crisis, but it's not automatic. You have to qualify as one of his family. This doesn't happen through church attendance, donating to worthy causes, or *doing* anything. It happens because you put your trust in what Jesus did for you 2,000 years ago. This confidence which erases fears is available to anybody. Most don't accept it because it requires humility. Our pride is firmly entrenched to the point we don't even recognize most of our thinking and actions are directed by it.

How do we defeat it? The Bible says, "All have sinned...sin's penalty is death...Jesus offers a gift of eternal life through His death, burial, and resurrection...it's ours by faith when we repent (confess and turn from our self-directed ways)...pray. Tell God you're sorry and want His truth to run your life. Check our "Steps To Salvation" for a more detailed explanation.

Your crises may or may not diminish. But if you've trusted Jesus, you can count on Him being with you in your personal den of lions and fiery furnaces.

January 19, 2023

WIIFM*

Everywhere I look, there are Help Wanted signs. It seems that anyone who wants to work could find a job. It may be temporary until something you really want is available, but by not working, you're skills are getting rusty, technology is passing you by, and aside from your leaky bank account shrinking, you're placing yourself in the way of temptation. You've heard the saying that idle hands are the devil's workshop.

Temptations come in many forms and often we don't recognize them because they come in packaging attractive to us. We can find any number of things to waste time on instead of looking for work or honing our skills so we have something to offer a prospective employer.

When I was still working and had the responsibility of hiring new salespeople, I was flabbergasted by the "requirements" of many of the applicants. And this is partially the reason of the title of today's post: *What's In It For Me? When the right question should have been, "What can I do, how can I help you grow your business?" And this phenomenon happened a few years before COVID. It appears that we have become a society of takers instead of givers, users rather than creators.

The other contributor to today's title came from my morning reading in the Psalms, 103 specifically. One of the first questions job applicants ask has to do with benefits: how many holidays, sick time, etc? I'm old school, but it used to be that benefits were a reward for doing a good job. The better the worker, the better the benefits. This is especially true in a sales environment, where results are usually the primary measurement of your job performance.

When I read the word "benefits" in verse two, my mind started racing to put these thoughts on paper. For those looking for benefits, working or not, you won't find a better package than this: *"Bless the Lord O my soul, and forget none of His benefits; who pardons all your iniquities, who heals all your diseases; who redeems your life from the pit, who crowns you with lovingkindness and compassion; who satisfies your years with good things, so that your youth is renewed like the eagle.(v.2-5)"*

These may not be what you had in mind, but as good as worldly benefits are, they will be destroyed in the coming judgment. God's benefits are permanent. Our guilt from ALL sin is *pardoned*, our diseases are ALL *healed.* He has prepared a place in heaven for us (Jn. 14:2,3) where there will be no pain, mourning, crying, death (Rev. 21:4).

For those of us who know Jesus as Savior, these are promises we can take to the bank. We may not see all of these benefits— God doesn't heal everybody in their earthly bodies—this side of heaven. But your sins are pardoned...now, your life is redeemed from the pit...now. You are crowned with lovingkindness and compassion...now. And we don't have to work for it. It's a free gift from our Father. So we can say with the Psalmist *"Bless the Lord O my soul and all that is within me bless His holy name* (v.1)."

For those who are still on the fence about "this God stuff," it's not too late. Jesus Christ loves you in spite of your sin, but that sin has separated you from Him. It's not a permanent condition if you come to Him in humble repentance and honestly desire to do a one-eighty in the time you have left on earth. Otherwise, none of these benefits will be yours. Instead, you'll be in a dark place forever, alone, in agony, and remembering all the times you were invited or encouraged to seek Jesus and you rejected Him. Don't wait. Come to Him...now, while he may be found (Isa. 55:6).

In the appendix, *Steps to Salvation*, you'll find a detailed description of God's perspective, His grace offered to anyone who comes on His terms, and an assurance if you come humbly, He WILL receive you into His forever family.

And that's the answer to the question, What's in it for me?

January 24, 2023

Humility or Hypocrisy

"Many a man proclaims his own loyalty, but who can find a trustworthy man?" (Prov. 20:6). In today's world, one doesn't have to look very hard or far to find this statement from King Solomon, the wisest man who ever lived (I Kings 4:30, 31), true.

Doesn't it push your buttons when our elected officials say or do one thing for (to) their constituents, and then exempt themselves? Whether it's true or just lore, George Washington is said to have stated, "I cannot tell a lie" when confronted with an axed cherry tree. Oh that we still had that kind of morality in our leaders.

I compiled a short list of synonyms for *hypocrisy (hypocrite)* along with the definition: "The practice of claiming to have moral standards or beliefs to which one's own behavior does not conform." Synonyms: phony, fraud, insincere, deceitful, deceptive, dishonest, falsely pious, sanctimonious. There are more. Anybody you know fit this description? Would you vote for them again?

Hypocrisy, per se, is not the problem. It's a symptom of a much deeper character flaw caused by consistent rejection of truth for personal gain. If you don't believe that, do your own research on how many senators and congressmen came to congress with relatively little net worth and compare it to their net worth now. I'm not suggesting they did anything illegal. But it does raise eyebrows.

Juxtapose the following definition of humility with that of hypocrisy: "a modest or low view of one's own importance." Doesn't that sound like a person who could be trusted? In general, let alone to represent his/her constituency.

It seems unnecessary to have to point out how far our nation has fallen into self-centeredness. It's not just our leaders, it's everywhere. Anyone who loves truth can see it. Our last post (WIIFM) scratched the surface and suggested that our focus is wrong. Today, let's look a little deeper into the root cause for lying and hypocrisy.

The following are God's opinions, not mine. I'm just the messenger. Don't shoot me.

"*You destroy those who speak **lies**. The Lord **loathes** the person of* bloodshed *and **deceit*** (Ps.5:6)".

"*One who practices **deceit** will not dwell within my house; one who* speaks **lies** *shall not maintain his position before me* (Ps. 101:7)".

"*Six things the Lord **hates**, seven that are an **abomination** to Him: ...a* lying ***tongue**...a **false witness** who declares **lies**...*(Prov. 6:16-19)".

"*A false witness **will not go unpunished**, and one who declares lies* will **perish** (Prov. 19:9)".

I realize that not everyone reading this takes the Bible literally. Spoiler alert: God does. And these verses are warnings to those of us who make lying and deceit a **way of life**. Look at the highlighted words: hates, loathes, abomination, will not go unpunished, will perish. Not words associated with a soft-hearted, grandfather-type who looks the other way when his children disobey. These warnings could not be more serious. They warn us of a permanent, eternal destiny apart from anything good.

Hypocrisy is a choice based on wrong motives, wrong thinking, self-centeredness. Any counselor worth his salt will tell you that you can't treat symptoms. It's just like pulling weeds. You have to get to the root. In this case the root is rejection of Jesus Christ and His claim on our lives. Until that issue is dealt with, the lies and hypocrisy will continue. God will never force anyone to stop their wrong choices. But He does offer a pretty compelling alternative.

Our title implies choice. Humility vs. hypocrisy. We've seen the fruits of hypocrisy. Let's look at the others. If we want the kind of life filled with peace, love, and all the good things God offers His children, we must believe and take His word seriously. The Bible is God's user's manual, given to introduce us to Him, His plan for our future, His promises when we obey, and His "correction" when we don't. Through it we are introduced to Jesus Christ, God in the flesh, and our ONLY way to know, love, and see God when we die.

The Bible says we sin (Rom. 3:23). Sin causes our death (Rom. 6:23). Jesus came to earth to die in our place (Rom. 5:8). **In Christ**, we are new creations, viewed as sinless by God (Rom. 8:1-12; 2 Cor. 5:17). This gift is available to all who come humbly to Jesus (John 6:37). There are no qualifications (i.e. money, education, good deeds, etc.) needed on your part. Just humble yourself and recognize you can't do it on your own. You NEED Jesus. For more detailed information, see the appendix *Steps to Salvation* in the back of this book. Hope to see you on the other side.

February 7, 2023

Doers Do

"Is there no end to windy words?" (Spoken by Job to his *"miserable comforters"* after they had sat silent for seven days, then laid into him with all kinds of erroneous charges as to the reason he was suffering [Job 16: 2,3]). It reminds me of our current political circus. Which is the point of today's thoughts.

As I was reading in Romans a couple days ago, I read this verse in 2:13, *"for it is **not the hearers** of the law who are righteous before God **but the doers** of the law who will be justified."* It got me wondering what else God had to say about this topic. I found a few. James 1:22, *"But prove yourselves **doers of the word**, and **not just hearers who deceive themselves.**"* And another from Psalm 111:10, *"The fear of the Lord is the beginning of wisdom, a good understanding have **all those** who **do His commandments.**"* There are more, but you get the drift.

Solomon adds a crowning touch in Prov. 10:19, *"When there are many words, transgression is unavoidable, but he who restrains his lips is wise."* I've often wished that politicians could get to the meat of their speech without all the posturing and pontificating before the point is made. There is a direct relationship between "many words" and those who hear but do nothing. The Bible says they (the hearers) deceive themselves. The question I ask, "Is that the intent of many words, to deceive the hearers?" Hmm. Could that also be the reason many of our proposed laws come in volumes of 2,000 pages or more; nobody is expected to read them…before the vote?

Fake news is a relatively recent term added to our vocabulary. It's often tied to the media, but aside from their bias toward one side of the aisle, don't they get their talking points from their favorite politicians? Years ago, I was taught in sales and in writing to be direct, to use one-syllable words instead of multi-syllable words when you can. They get the thought across faster and with less chance of error.

So, with all that as background, my goal is to encourage the reader to take stock of your life. Do you sit in the pew, hear the words, but go your way the same as you were when you walked in the door? That's a waste of your time. God's word is written for us and is *"profitable for teaching, for reproof, for correction, for training in righteousness* (2 Tim. 3:16). We are not to hear and do nothing. If we want to be blessed by God, we need to be *"**doers** of the law"*. James also says (1:25), *"But one who...continued* (in the law) *not having become a **forgetful hearer** but an **active doer**...will be blessed in what he does."*

Do we want God's blessing? It's offered to *all* who do it His way. The starting point is to change our thinking. Every act is preceded by a thought. We're told in Romans 12:2, *"Do not be conformed to this world but be transformed by the **renewing of your mind**, so that you may prove what the will of God is, that which is good and acceptable and perfect."*

The world looks at us Christians with a critical eye to see if our words line up with our actions. When we hear (or speak or write) but don't do, we stoke their fire of judgment of us and their label of hypocrite isn't too far off the mark. Let's make today the day we allow the Holy Spirit to have all of us, especially the inner thoughts and motives that drive our doing, not because it earns salvation, but because we love Jesus and are grateful for all He's done for us.

If you're reading this and it has caused you to react defensively, it could be that you are in the camp who has heard the truth of the gospel, maybe for years, but not done anything about it. Reread paragraph 2 above. James says you have deceived yourself. It's not too late to become a new creation (2 Cor. 5:17) in Christ. Don't wait. Time is short and Jesus could call us home any day. For a detailed look at what God thinks of your condition and the steps to have a relationship with Him, Read our *Steps To Salvation* appendix in the back of this book.

Thanks for reading.

July 23, 2023

Deliver The Mail

Neither snow nor rain nor heat nor gloom of night…are the beginning words of the unofficial motto of the U.S. Postal Service. They're supposed to imply the commitment to do all in the postal carrier's ability to get your letter or package to you. But in today's world of shortages, ambivalence, excuses, and more, their reputation has suffered.

They say necessity is the mother of invention. I think that's why such an opportunity for companies like FedEx, UPS, and Amazon (who sometimes has same-day delivery) exists. "Find a need and fill it" is the first rung on the business ladder of success.

Fortunately for those of us who are involved in sharing our faith in Jesus Christ, we are not held accountable for "success" in spreading the gospel of Jesus' death and resurrection. We are only commanded to "deliver the mail" so to speak. Go. Tell. These are action verbs intended to provide direction to God's children when they ask the question, "What is God's will for me?".

This should be the only encouragement we need to get off the couch and into the battle for souls. In this world, we are judged by our accomplishments. How big is our bank account? How new is our car? Do we wear designer clothes? We are constantly bombarded by media soundbites accusing us of not keeping up with the Joneses, hammering at our dissatisfaction and attempting to guilt us into spending money for their product.

In God's world, we are privileged to carry the truth of eternity to a lost and dying population. Many won't want to hear it. Don't let that discourage you to the point of quitting. We are not responsible for results, reactions, or rejections. They are rejecting Jesus, not you. Life is a breath. Eternity comes in the blink of an eye when a decision for Jesus is too late. We only have to please the audience of One by our obedience.

Keep the faith. Depend on the Holy Spirit for the right words at the right time. If we don't speak, the stones will cry out (Luke 19:40). If we deliver the mail, when we get to heaven we can expect to hear "well done."

September 15, 2023

To or From

Little words with tremendous implications. Opposite directional words that expose our hearts, belie our attitudes, and condemn or confirm us. Jesus said to the people gathered around, "So if the Son makes you free, you will be free indeed" (Jn. 8:36). The question we should be asking is, "free from what?"

Many people who have been exposed to the good news of Jesus and have made an intellectual decision to "be a Christian," seem to think it is freedom *to* continue their sinful ways, that God will overlook their sin because they've "gotten their ticket punched." But consider our title today. Scripture is very clear that we who have embraced Jesus' death and resurrection and received new life in Him are free *from* our sin and guilt: freedom *from* sin, NOT freedom *to* sin.

Paul, in Romans 5:20 – 6:2 spells it out plainly: "…where sin increased grace abounded all the more…Are we to continue in sin so that grace may increase? May it never be! How shall we who died to sin still live in it?"

As we see "the day" drawing near (Heb. 10:25), our focus should be on staying awake and alert to *our* readiness to meet Jesus and to His command to "sanctify Christ as Lord in your hearts, always being ready to make a defense to everyone who asks you to give an account for the hope that is in you, but with gentleness and respect" (I Pet.3:15). In other words, live your life in such a way as to invite people to ask why you're different, and then tell them about how Jesus loves them and they can have the same peace you have, knowing where you'll spend eternity.

Let's go back to our directional words for today. Life is a continuum from the day we're born to the day we die. We can generally tell by looking at people, where they are on that continuum. But we're also on a spiritual continuum and our location is not as important as our direction. Are we heading *to* or *from* the God who created the universe and gave us life? Is our sin (for the most part) in our rearview mirror or beckoning us to the horizon in front of us? Time on earth is getting shorter every day and we don't know when God will call us out of the game.

In Matthew, Jesus was talking to His disciples about when He would return to gather His church (all believers) and He warned them, "For this reason you also must be ready; for the Son of Man is coming at an hour when you do not think He will" (Matt. 24:44). Why would He say that? First of all, it's a good principle for life in general. We need to be ready for a lot of things: ready for work or school, ready for traffic mishaps, ready for moving day, etc. But more importantly, Jesus knew that man is prone to go down rabbit trails and forget the time. In the spiritual world, since we can't visibly see into it, it's truly a faith-walk that needs encouragement, reminders, motivation to stay the course, and more.

While you consider whether you're a *to* or a *from* pilgrim today, remember that when we gave control of our lives to Jesus, at that moment, we became new creatures with the Holy Spirit living in us and the power to live a victorious life that is pleasing to God. No longer are we bound by sinful habits that seem to have a chokehold on us. WE ARE FREE in Christ.

If you don't feel free, If you're still in bondage to some particular sin, go to God in prayer and confess it. You may also have to find an accountability partner you can share your journey with and mutually encourage each other. Perhaps memorizing this verse will help: "Therefore if anyone is in Christ, he is a new creature; the old things passed away behold, new things have come" (II Cor. 5:17). God doesn't lie. So if you're in Christ, you're a new creature, free *from* sin and its consequences. Free *to* follow Jesus.

Hope this has been an encouragement to stay the course until we see Jesus. It could be any day now.

November 13 2023
No I in Team

We've all heard the coach's pep talk, "There's no I in TEAM" intended to build camaraderie among team members and a reminder to not be a ball hog. We may have heard the same thing in a business environment where it or something like it—"We all work for the same company here"—is preached if not practiced.

Generally speaking, an organization will perform better if everybody has that mindset. If you're very good at what you do, let your results speak for themselves. Nobody likes arrogance or boastful pride. But I want us to consider just where we—or in line with this topic, "I"—fit in.

The other day, I was musing over the placement of the letter I in two words that have nearly opposite meanings. I only noticed it because I made a typo and my word processing software didn't catch it because both were legitimate words. The words: complaint and compliant.

For sure, in our society today, we have much that we could offer complaint about; ranging from politics (especially) to citizen activist anger to world unrest for which there seems no solution. But ask yourself these questions: Where did it come from? Why now at this time in world history? Why does it seem to be everywhere on the world stage? Is there anything besides war that can fix it?

As with everything I write, my sole source for truth is the Word of God, the Bible. True to form, we find the answer there: *"Why should any living mortal or any man offer complaint in view of his sins?* (Lam. 3:39)"and *"Do all things without complaining or arguments* (Phil.2:14)"*. With the number of verses that mention complaining, it must be important to God.

When we complain, it's the equivalent of an accusation against God that He doesn't know what He's doing or He's not watching or aware of what's impacting me. Is that really where you want to be? More backup: *"And we know that God causes all things to work together for good to those who love God, to those who are called according to His purpose"* (Rom.8:28). And *"...God is faithful, who will not allow you to be tempted beyond what you are able..."* (I Cor. 10:31).

Having said that, do not infer I am saying that being compliant is an all-inclusive category that we must bend the knee to. Yes, God tells us to obey the government (Tit. 3:1), but not if their rules violate God's law. He also gives examples of how to approach rulers in humility to achieve our goal. Spoiler alert: It doesn't include civil disturbance, rioting and looting.

The answer to the questions above is not found in politics, or the classroom, or in gender modification, but in a heart transplant. *"I will give you a new heart, and a new spirit I will put within you. And I will remove the heart of stone from your flesh and give you a heart of flesh.* (Ezek. 36:26).

If you haven't experienced this heart transplant from the One who created your heart and promises that *"…if anyone is in Christ, he is a new creation; the old things passed away; behold, new things have come…"*—and this includes a new heart—hear what Jesus says to you: *"He who comes to me I will never cast out."* (John 6:37).

This post gives you a simplistic example of how big a difference putting "I" in the wrong place can make in just the definition of a word. Ask yourself "Am 'I' in the right place (with Jesus) so that when I die, for sure I'll be in the right place."

If you don't know Jesus Christ as your personal Savior and Lord and where you'll spend eternity and you want to but don't know how, turn to the section "Steps to Salvation" for a simple explanation of how to meet Jesus.

If you do know Jesus as Savior and Lord, there's someone in your sphere of influence that doesn't. Suit up it's time to share the gospel with them. I hope to see you there.

January 19, 2024
Hope or Hype?

I wrote about hope back in September 2021 (*Hope Does Not Disappoint*), but at the beginning of this new year, it seems a fitting topic to be revisited because hopelessness today seems more prevalent than two and a half years ago. What has happened in that time? Several things come to mind. We have a different political team leading America. Russia invaded Ukraine in February of 2022, almost two years ago. On October 7, 2023, Hamas militants, unprovoked, attacked Israel. If you've followed either of these two atrocities, you've seen the picture of hopelessness on the faces of those affected by them.

Hope is realistic only if it's tied to a high probability of being true. Las Vegas exists because of hope. And it survives and builds bigger and bigger casinos because of it. You've seen the ads: "Loosest Slots" "Big Winners" etc. But how many come home with their hope of striking it big realized? If the majority did, all the neon of Vegas would soon be dark, just a memory. That's reality.

Life has to have hope or we become depressed, susceptible to addictive behavior, or suicidal. We hope for a raise, a winning lottery ticket, kids who are good students, good athletes, and more. But our society is becoming more and more hopeless because we have put our hope in the hype of politics and politicians. Hope makes us want to believe the lies for a better future if we'll just "get in line and follow 'The Plan' espoused by our leaders."

For decades, we have watched our moral standards slip away into the depths of selfishness, wokeism, inane group-think and behavior, and politicians who seem to have lost all touch with reality. According to the 2nd law of thermodynamics, chaos never reverts to order without a major reboot, i.e. something of such magnitude as to change the very system in which the chaos exists. Just such a change is on the horizon. This shouldn't be a surprise to those of us who read and believe what God said millennia ago.

Remember the worldwide flood of Noah's day? Their society had become so wretched that God's observation as penned by Moses in Genesis 6:5-8 was, "Then the Lord saw that the wickedness of man was great on the earth, and that every intent of the thoughts of his heart was only evil continually. The Lord was sorry that He had made man on the earth and He was grieved in His heart. The Lord said, 'I will blot out man whom I have created from the face of the land, from man to animals to creeping things and to birds of the sky; for I am sorry that I have made them.' But Noah found favor in the eyes of the Lord."

Ask yourself, "Is the day we're living in so different than then?" Let's look again at God's perspective as recorded by Paul in Romans 1:18-28 "For the wrath of God is revealed from heaven against all ungodliness and unrighteousness of men, who suppress the truth in unrighteousness, because what can be known about God is evident within them, for God made it evident to them...they are without excuse...for even though they knew God, they did not honor Him as God or give thanks, but they became futile in their speculations, and their foolish heart was darkened. Professing to be wise, they became fools, and exchanged the glory of the incorruptible God for an image in the form of corruptible man and of birds and four-footed animals and crawling creatures. Therefore God gave them over...to impurity...to degrading passions...to a depraved mind...to do those things which are not proper..."

God's patience is legendary. There are examples of God giving His people hundreds of years to come back to Him and abandon their godless lifestyles. But, and this is crucial, His patience has a limit. In the verses above, "God gave them over" is a phrase implying judgment. There are several types of judgment. One is physical. Ananias and Sapphira were judged for lying to Peter (and the Holy Spirit) and dropped dead instantly. King Nebuchadnezzar was made to eat grass and live like an animal for seven years until he recognized that God, not him, was in charge.

Another is spiritual. If we don't give up our sinful, godless lives, our eternal future is sealed in hell, "If anyone worships the beast and his image, and receives a mark on his forehead or on his hand, he also will drink of the wine of the wrath of God, which is mixed in full strength in the cup of His anger; and he will be tormented with fire and brimstone in the presence of the holy angels and in the presence of the Lamb. And the smoke of their torment goes up forever and ever; they have no rest day and night..."

This is a picture of a time on earth called "The Tribulation", a time when God has removed all true believers from earth to begin our eternity with Jesus in heaven. Those who are still on earth are those who have rejected Christ during their lifetime and are experiencing God's wrath ("natural" disasters on a worldwide scale; fires everywhere, 1/3 of the rivers and oceans will be turned to blood (Rev. 8:9,10), and much more) is being poured out on the earth and all who have rejected Jesus as the only way to a permanent relationship with God.

So how does all this doom and gloom relate to hope? If you're reading this, then you haven't passed the point of no return. There is nothing you have done, no attitude or action, which is beyond the reach of God's mercy. There is just one requirement. You have to humble yourself and come to God on His terms (through Jesus Christ's death and resurrection). Recognize that you are a sinner and literally have nothing good in yourself to offer a holy God. If you can do this, then, go to the section in this book, *Steps To Salvation* and follow the outline.

If you think you've committed an unpardonable sin and are concerned about it, you haven't. It's if you don't care and think this is all a bunch of hooey that you're in trouble. The hope you can cling to is that God loves you, Jesus died to pay for your godlessness, and there is forgiveness ONLY IN JESUS CHRIST. It's not Jesus plus good deeds, Jesus plus baptism, Jesus plus giving money. Literally, it's Jesus plus nothing…except your humility and confession of sin. I have hope that you will take this seriously and allow God's Spirit to speak to your heart before it's too late. Thanks for reading.

January 25, 2024
The Three Rs

We've all heard of the Three Rs from school days, Reading, wRiting, and aRithmetic. But do you know the Three Rs from Revelation? Remember, Repent, and Return (implied) (Rev. 2:5). Alliteration is often a useful tool to help us remember key points in the written word, speeches, or debates. I use it here because what I want you to remember is one of the most important things you could have in your life's arsenal to combat the evil wiles of your biggest adversary.

In the first three chapters of Revelation, John relates the message he got from Jesus Himself to the seven churches of the first century. The message hasn't changed and is applicable for modern churches as it was then.

The church at Ephesus, from all outward appearances, had their act together. They challenged and rejected false teachers. They refused to tolerate evil. But over a period of about 40 years, when the next generation had taken over, the motivating force behind their acts had waned. Their love of Jesus had become cold and they were going through the motions in a mechanical orthodoxy. "The loss of a vital love relationship with the Lord Jesus Christ opened the doors to spiritual apathy, indifference to others, love for the world, compromise with evil, judgment, and ultimately, the death of the church altogether."[1]

Jesus warned them, as God had to do with the Israelites many times throughout the Old Testament, that they "had left their first love." He was very clear when asked "which is the great commandment in the Law?" (Matt. 22:36-38). He said, "You shall love the Lord your God with all your heart, and with all your soul, and with all your mind." This was the big sin the church at Ephesus was guilty of. And if you look closely at many churches today, they are guilty of the same thing, doing it all by rote, not because the love of Jesus compels them to "love God and love your neighbor."

What was the consequence of not returning to "do the deeds you did at first"? Their lampstand would be removed (representative of judgment) and they would be a dead church. If you find yourself in this situation, there's time to respond to the same message: Remember, Repent, Return, before it's too late. Jesus also said, "…he who comes to Me, I will never cast out" (John 6:37).

---

[1] MacArthur New Testament Commentary

February 9, 2024
Countdown Clock

The world of marketing and advertising creates a *false* sense of urgency with phrases like: "Only 14 left at this price," "Sale ends at midnight," "Be the envy of your neighborhood" and anything else they can concoct around the themes of limited time, limited number, limited pricing, to get you to buy something you don't need, with money you don't have, to impress people you don't even know or care about.

In the real world, there are deadlines you need to meet or there is some kind of penalty; late fees, disqualification, miss the flight, etc. Usually, you can live with the penalty. A little more money. A delay to your trip. And so on. Irritating? Yes. Life and death? Not usually.

But there is an offer with a deadline you for sure do not want to miss. The Bible tells us to "Seek the Lord while He may be found; call upon Him (for salvation) while He is near" (Isa. 55:6). I know many of you reading this know and love the Lord Jesus Christ. But I also know there are those who don't give a rip about Jesus, or, worse yet, think they're saved but aren't. This warning is for the second group.

For over 2,000 years since Jesus walked the earth, we have been reminded that He *is* coming back to earth. Isaiah is implying that there will come a time when men will look for Him and not find Him. When will that be? Nobody knows, but we have signs that indicate the time could be close. What's the penalty for missing *this* deadline? Eternity separated from God in a place nobody in their right mind would want to be: hell, a place that the Bible calls the Lake of Fire, where there will be weeping and gnashing of teeth.

There are two reasons this may happen. First, you'll die before you decide to let Jesus control your life. Second, Jesus will return to take His people (the church) home to heaven. Before either of those happen, while you still have breath, it's not too late. Once either happens, it's over. The Bible says, "…it is appointed for men to die once, and after this comes judgment" (Heb.9:27).

Heaven is a place where no sin exists. There will be no liars, cheats, bullies, or Satan to disturb the perfect peace and harmony created by God for His children to enjoy…forever. It will be like the beauty of Hawaii, the majesty of the Rocky Mountains (or the Alps), the serenity of Yosemite after an early Spring snow…forever. We earthlings can't even imagine all the good things that God has planned for us. I urge you to read the *Steps To Salvation* elsewhere in this book.

February 16, 2024
Today's Headline From 2500 Years Ago

It doesn't take a rocket scientist to know something is wrong with our society. But it does take intellectual honesty. The United States was founded on Biblical principles; our Founding Fathers came here to escape religious persecution from the English crown. But in the last two and a half centuries, we have travelled so far down the slippery slope of worldliness that we can barely see the residual of our Christian roots.

Consider a couple of our laws. It's illegal to steal, illegal to murder. Why? Where did we get that idea? They were part of a group of 10, given to Moses by God Himself. In Moses' day, both carried severe penalties. Today, not so much. How have we deteriorated to the point where these two (and many others) are often winked at and rarely punished with "an eye for an eye" thinking instead of thinking perps are victims (of something).

I was reading in Daniel this morning and came across the answer. Although written around 530 BC, it answers the above question with specificity likely to be rejected by most in today's "anything goes" society. Most people don't like the idea of accountability to a Creator God who sets the rules. But see if the word to Israel then and the Church today isn't spot on: "…*all this calamity has come on us; yet we have not sought the favor of the Lord our God by **turning from our iniquity and giving attention to Your truth**. Therefore the Lord has kept the calamity in store and brought it on us…but we have not obeyed His voice* (Dan. 9:13,14; emphasis added).

Is it too late for America? No, it's never too late as long as we breathe. But the answer is one that not many will be willing to do. Hear God's heart toward His people: (2 Chronicles 7:13-14 NASB) – "***If I** shut up the heavens so that there is no rain, or **if I** command the locust to devour the land, or **if I** send a plague among My people, **and My people** who are called by My name **humble themselves**, and **pray** and **seek My face**, and **turn from their wicked ways**, **then I will** hear from heaven, and **I will** forgive their sin and (I)will heal their land.*" Notice this is written to God's people, not the world at large.

What computer software can do is amazing. But there's one basic command that follows a specific rule: If-Then. **If** you want a certain outcome, **then** you have to follow the specific rule. God's promise is more sure than a computer *if-then* statement. We want healing for our land? Simple: 1) humble ourselves, 2) pray, 3) seek God, 4) turn from our wicked ways. We can't blame God for our problems. We only have to look in a mirror to find the source.

What will it take to stop hoping that electing the "right" politicians, and "tolerating" all kinds of aberrant behavior will somehow return us to a state of peace and serenity with no fear to walk my neighborhood at night? For the person who is willing to do the four steps outlined above, you will see the change you hope for in your own life and attain the *"peace of God which surpasses all comprehension..."* (Phil.4:7). That's the secret, but also the problem.

Most people reading this won't do what is necessary to change themselves and thereby change society. The second law of thermodynamics supports this: (paraphrased) all things in an "isolated system" degenerate into a more disordered state (entropy). That's why man and his grand (and expensive) plans to control climate variances by passing laws and enacting unproven limits on society will only tax and aggravate the members and never accomplish their goals. Everything moves from order to chaos, never the other way around.

Something to think about: If God punishes His people when they disobey Him, how much more will he punish those who reject Him? Thanks for reading.

March 26, 2024
Now and Later

Two buildings stand side by side, separated by a wide moat filled with large allegators. On top of the first is a treasure nobody has ever seen, riches beyond comprehension. On top of the second building are lots of people, music, laughter and, though not immediately apparent from below, loneliness.

You approach with a ladder that will reach the top of the second building, but not the top of the first. You see a label on the second: "NOW". The taller building is labeled "LATER".

There is a man standing at the base of the first building, dressed in stained work clothes, and holding a sign that says, "Leave your baggage here and I will help you reach the top." You look at him and think, "he doesn't have a ladder, this must be a scam. Besides, it looks like everybody else is 'over there'".

There's also a man dressed in fine clothes, with a sign, at the bottom of the second building that reads, "Free ticket to the top." It seems like a no-brainer, so you plant your ladder and begin the ascent.

As you step from rung to rung, you begin to hear what sounds like sobbing, though nothing loud enough to mask the gaiety you believe to be up there. You keep going, step, step, step. You pass a sign that says "one way only" and wonder what that could possibly mean. You find the climb is longer than you thought and pause to rest.

Glancing at the other building, you notice a stairway you hadn't seen before and an older man being helped up by the 'worker'. But you still can't see the top. Although you begin to faintly hear what sounds like an orchestra and choir. Hmm. As you near the top, the sobbing grows in intensity and you hear people yelling at each other. You begin to think, "what's going on?" but you keep going step, step, step.

You look again at the other building and notice that the higher the two men go, the less the worker has to help the older man. He seems to have more energy, a quicker step. But you conclude your eyes are playing tricks on you because you're becoming tired and keep going.

Upon reaching the top, you discover an easy transition from your ladder to the roof in the form of a platform hanging with an opening in the parapet. You step off your ladder and immediately someone pushes your ladder away from the building and it falls to the ground below. You asked the person who pushed the ladder why he did that. He reminded you of the one way sign you noticed on the way up.

You quickly understand that all the sounds you heard were from a series of concert-type speakers. There is nobody there. You are roughly grabbed by two large grotesque beings and immediately wrapped in chains with locks even Superman couldn't open. As you pass an opening to your cell, you notice a sign overhead, "Abandon hope all ye who enter here."*

Just before you are thrown into your cell, you hear the most beautiful music and singing you've ever heard coming from the roof of the other building. And you know you made the wrong choice.

Friends, this is a graphic picture of the choice we face **before we die**. The God who created heaven and earth has lovingly given us untold chances to "choose the right building." The Bible says in Romans, *"that which is known about God is evident within them* [unrighteous men]; *for God made it evident to them. For since the creation of the world His invisible attributes, His eternal power and divine nature, have been clearly seen, being understood through what has been made, **so that they are without excuse.***

To be clear, Jesus is the building labeled 'Later'. He said, *"...the one who comes to Me I certainly will not cast out."* The only way to reach the top is through Jesus. He also said, *"I am the way and the truth and the life, no one comes to the Father but through Me."* Have you come to Jesus yet? If so, you're assured a place at the top of the right building. If not, it's not too late. In the back of this book is a section titled "Steps to Salvation." Make sure you read that before the day is over. Tomorrow is not guaranteed to anyone.

*From Dante's Inferno

March 31, 2024
Again and Again

My reading today brought me to the Old Testament book of Judges. Haven't been here for quite a while. But just the name often strikes fear when I think I might have to stand before one for something stupid I did.

The book starts out as a continuation of where Joshua left off right after his death. If you remember, Joshua had led an exemplary life. He was one of two spies (Caleb was the other) that were sent to spy out the land God had promised and came back with a faith-filled "let's do it" attitude to attack. The other ten spies had a fear-filled report and convinced all the people everyone would die if they fought. Well, it cost the doubters entrance into the Promised Land because God became angry and would have wiped them out had it not been for Moses' intervention.

The first four chapters of Judges tell how the Israelites "did evil in the sight of the Lord" again and again. A key verse is in Judges 2:2,3 *"But you have not obeyed Me…Therefore…"*. And God follows up with what He's going to do to punish them. There is another key verse a few later, *"there arose another generation after them who did not know the Lord, nor yet the work which He had done for Israel. (v10)"*

Two things jump out at me in this section. First, God's extreme patience with Israel's sin and rejection of Him. Five times in these chapters, we see specifically the charge against them "they did evil…". And five times, they called out to God and He bailed them out.

The second thing, and perhaps the lesson for us today, is in verse 10. Obviously, the parents hadn't trained the next generation in the ways of the Lord. Look at the outcome, *"they did evil…served the Baals…forsook the Lord…act more corruptly than their fathers. (v11-19)"*

When I view our society today, the same charges apply to us, evil, idolatry, turn our back on God, more corrupt than last generation. I'm not a history scholar, but I do know the 2nd law of thermodynamics: everything moves from order to chaos. Think back to the 50s and 60s or even further, the 30s and 40s. Yes there was evil in the world. And, yes there was idolatry and more. But there was also a sense of right and wrong, a morality that kept society more in check. Where has that gone?

God has not changed in the millennia since Joshua's era. Judgment is upon us because we have become exactly like early Israel. Most people don't make the connection between our behavior and the chaos in the world. It's because they don't have a relationship with the One who makes the rules, the One who *"is the same yesterday, today and forever* (Heb. 13:8)".

We can be thankful that God *is* the same. His amazing patience and love haven't morphed into a distant, unapproachable judge who's waiting for our execution. But there is one thing we would have to do that most won't: turn from our self-centered existence, in humility, and agree that we've broken the rules (the Bible calls it sin). If we do that before it's too late, God promises forgiveness. Jesus said, *"the one who comes to me I certainly will not cast out (John 6:37)"*. He also said, *"I am the way and the truth and the life, no one comes to the Father but through Me (John 14:6)"*.

It's simple. We have to do it His way. But His way is the way to an eternal relationship with God, filled with peace and life beyond our comprehension in a place prepared for His children. If we don't, there's "the other place" described as filled with "darkness and weeping and gnashing of teeth" (Matt. 13:50). While you still breathe, you have time to decide. Don't wait. Tomorrow is not guaranteed to anyone.

Today is Easter. Christians all over the world celebrate because this day is the guarantee that God's promises are all true and available to all. More than 500 eye-witnesses saw Jesus, talked with Him, and ate with Him after the resurrection. To deny that is to seal your fate in "the other place." Please don't.

May 2, 2024
If Not Me…

The other day, I was with a group of men studying the Beatitudes in Matthew. You know, blessed are the…fill in the blank. Just after that section we're reminded that we are salt and light. Our study took us through the primary attributes of both. It was a convicting study because of the one glaring conclusion I came away with. And it's represented in today's title. The missing part, the convicting part comes after the ellipsis: *Then Who?*

I don't mean this to be a diatribe against today's religious system, but when the facts about salt and light are considered and applied to our lives, it can't help but sting just a little.

In my book, *Christ in Men…Today (Brokenness, pg. 32),* I referred to Rebecca Manley Peppert's book *Out of the Salt Shaker & into the World.* Her point is simple. Salt doesn't do any good while it's in the shaker. If we wait until our shaker is polished and shiny before we share the gospel with anyone, our motive is wrong. When we want something salted, we don't care what the shaker looks like.

And what about "light"? Jesus told His listeners (my paraphrase), "You don't light a light and then cover it up. You place it where it can light up the room."

Fellow travelers, the Bible tells us we *are* salt and light. Are we comfortable in our shaker? Do we throw a blanket over our light? If we pass the entrance exam for admittance to heaven (faith in Jesus Christ alone), we are accountable to God for a life lived so salt and light are spread wherever we go, whatever we do.

How's that working in your life? Do people even know you're a Christian, I mean a living, breathing, fire eating representative of Jesus? If not, ask yourself WHY? Are you trying to fit it? Why? Do you not know enough? Why? You do know, don't you, that God will ask you these questions someday. Might want to have an answer prepared that doesn't sound like a lame excuse.

Today's thoughts are purposely short. The message is simple and, I hope, clear. I pray you'll ponder (I love that word) what I've said and take it to heart. Yes, Jesus forgives us when we don't "spread". But wouldn't it be better to amass rewards for doing it His way? Thanks for reading.

May 3, 2024
Competition is not a bad word.

In fact, when we use our God-given talents to be the best we can, we honor and glorify God. We often see the negative side of competition—the strutting and taunting—but that says more about the character of those who behave that way than about the act of competing.

I love it when scripture gives me an idea to write about, like it did today. I was in 2 Cor. 5:10, *"For we must all appear before the judgment seat of Christ, so that **each one may be recompensed** for his deeds in the body, **according to what he has done**, whether good or bad."* We know this has nothing to do with sin because of the little phrase "in the body." It's talking about the body of Christ. Our sin was taken care of at the cross. Nobody in the body has rejected Jesus as their savior. Generally, theologians agree that this means all the things we do *after* we're saved.

Then there's also Galatians 6:4, *"Each one must examine his own work, and then he will have reason for boasting in regard to himself and not in regard to another. For each one **will bear his own load**."*

On God's scorecard, there's only one name—yours. We are not measured by how well we do compared to "Bob". Did your parents or coach ever tell you how you were not living up to your *potential*? That's God's measuring stick too. How well are we doing compared to how well we could be doing if only…If only I had spent more time in the Word. If only I hadn't skimped on my giving. If only, if only, if only.

We might be able to get away with excuses with people who can't see inside us. Ironically, even though God is the only One who can see our hearts, He lets us think we can get away with excuses with Him…for a while. But when we appear before Him at the judgment seat, none of that will stand up.

One problem that plagues many Christians is we're not satisfied with the gifts, skills, and talents God has personally chosen for us. We focus on what Bob has that we don't and we're tempted to whine. What does that say to God about our gratitude for what we *do* have? We need to do an assessment of our abilities and work on strengthening them. You ask, "How do I do that?" The same way you build muscles. You use them. If you have the gift of service, you serve. The gift of giving? Give. Stretch. Reach. Set bigger and bigger goals.

We are only in competition with ourselves. And, like muscles that atrophy through non-use, our unused gifts will atrophy too. The verse above says, "each one will be recompensed for his deeds." What does that mean? It means "to give something to by way of compensation." We understand that, because we work for a paycheck. But try to get your mind around obligating God to compensate us for our deeds. And then think about what kind of reward I would get for my bad deeds. Would it be something negative or would it just reduce the rewards I could have gotten if my good deeds were greater? Any answer I give would be speculation, because the Bible doesn't say more than it says.

Lest anyone misunderstand, I'm not promoting good deeds as a way to earn heaven. That only comes by trusting in Jesus alone to cover my sin. But the Bible clearly talks about our getting rewards in heaven. One verse that should excite all believers in Christ is Revelation 22:12, *"Behold, I am coming quickly, and My reward is with Me, to reward each one as his work deserves."* And God's encouragement to hang in there from Galatians 6:9, *"Let us not lose heart in doing good, for **in due time** we will reap if we do not grow weary."*

It might be good to ponder these verses and ask yourself, "Do I deserve, or have I done anything to earn a reward?" There's still time to impact the good vs. bad balance. God gifted us for service. The Bible says, "...**as He wills**" (1 Cor. 12:11). When we're tempted to grump about our gifting compared to others, remember this verse. Our job is to use the gift(s) we've been given—everybody has at least one spiritual gift—for God's glory, not our own. Beware. Pride lurks.

We started out talking about competition and how the world sees it. I hope you now have a little different perspective on how God views it and what you can still do to tip the scales in your favor. Thanks for reading.

May 30, 2024
There Are Answers

But nobody is asking the right questions. What should I study in school to have a good career? Where should I live? What kind of car should I buy? These are all *good* questions. But in the big picture, they're not important.

The value of these questions is dependent on your world view. If you're one who believes things like "there is no God" or "I'm in control of my life" or the worst one, "I'll think about God when I'm settled in a career, married, and have a family," then this post is especially for you.

So what is the right question? The most important question you need to answer is, "Where will I spend eternity?" I know many don't believe there is anything after death. And there are those that believe all religions lead to God. And still others believe that because they've led a "good" life, God will have to let them into heaven.

If you've read any of my other posts, you know that the only "proof text" I use is the Bible. If you don't accept this book as the inspired, infallible, inerrant word of God, then you won't buy any of my arguments. But if you're openly searching for truth, then you're in the right place. Keep reading.

The first step on this path is to accept the fact that there is a God. The Bible says, *"In the beginning, God…"* (Gen. 1:1) The beginning of what? Time. Hours, days, years, etc. It's hard to wrap our minds around anything that transcends time because it's all we know. We're born. We live so many years. We die. The first step of faith is to believe in the right God. But that step is not blind. You just have to look around to see God either in or behind everything.

The rest of the first verse of the Bible says, *"…created the heavens and the earth."* Belief in the statistically impossible rather than belief in the living God, doesn't seem to make sense; that something as intricate and marvelous as our universe evolved from slime. Even if that was true, where did the slime come from? And isn't it a lot more reasonable to believe in an all-powerful, all-knowing God who designed creation then spoke it into existence, than that everything that lives plants, animals and especially humans evolved from the same slime?

The Bible says, *"For the wrath of God is revealed from heaven against all ungodliness and unrighteousness of men who suppress the truth in unrighteousness, because that which is known about God is evident within them; for God made it evident to them. For since the creation of the world His invisible attributes, His eternal power and divine nature, have been clearly seen, being understood through what has been made, so that they are without excuse."* (Rom. 1:18-20)

You don't have to look any farther than your bathroom mirror. The crowning glory of God's creation is staring back at you. Take any part of your body: eyes, nose, hands, you pick. Now consider the anatomical functions of the body, all controlled by the brain. And what about the body's self-healing properties? Evolution? It takes a lot of denial of the obvious to believe in some of the presuppositions of the theory of evolution..

The next step is to embrace His Word, the Bible. Using men to actually pen the words inspired by the Holy Spirit, it took about 1,500 years to complete from the first book (Genesis) to the last book (Revelation). Every word was inspired by God the Holy Spirit. It is the only book (actually a collection of 66 books) written by around 40 men over many centuries, that never contradicts itself. The Bible says, *"Every word of God is tested; He is a shield to those who take refuge in Him."* (Prov. 30:5)

Every prophecy made in Scripture that has already been fulfilled, was fulfilled exactly. The measure of a prophet of God is 100% accuracy 100% of the time. That's why we can believe the prophecies made but not yet fulfilled. And there are many dealing with the final days of earth.

Let's move on. The Bible is very clear about life after death. It says, *"it is appointed for men to die once and after this comes judgment"* (Heb. 9:27) And another, *"**now** is the day of salvation"* (2 Cor. 6:2).

The Bible also confirms that there are only two destinations: heaven and hell. Just the descriptions of both should be enough to make our decision as to where we want to spend eternity. But, unfortunately, they don't. Why? Because heaven requires sacrifice, obedience, humility, and trust. Hell is our default and doesn't require anything. In fact, Satan would have you not ever think about heaven and hell.

Heaven requires that we trust the work of someone else to get our name on the list of attendees. This requires humility to agree that I'm not good enough to do it on my own. But more than that, just admitting that I'm not good enough is not good enough. We have to understand our plight as a sinner, repent, and plead our case to the Judge of the universe, Jesus Christ. He's the one who "did the work" that allows us into heaven. And that "work" was dying on a cross in our place. The Bible says, *"without the shedding of blood, there is no forgiveness."* (Heb. 9:22)

Why is that important? God is holy and cannot tolerate sin. We sin. It separates us from God. Heaven is where God is. As sinful beings (we are, regardless of how good we think we are), there's no way—on our own—to make it to heaven. Jesus said, *"I am the way and the truth and the life, no one comes to the Father but through Me."* (John 14:6). There is only **one way** to heaven. Good deeds aren't it. Big donations aren't either. Religions that teach Jesus plus anything are heresy. *"For by grace you have been saved through faith; and that not of yourselves, it is the gift of God; not as a result of works, so that no one may boast."* (Eph. 2:8,9)

Fortunately, God is a God of love and mercy. He designed a plan to allow us to be with Him forever. That plan was the death and resurrection of His Son, Jesus Christ.

The good news is that we have options. We can accept and believe that Jesus died for *my* sin and submit our lives to His substitutionary payment for it. Or we can reject that truth, go on our merry way, and end up in hell, regretting for eternity that we didn't take the free gift of life when available. Don't wait. When you breathe your last breath, it's over. Drop the curtain. Tomorrow is not guaranteed to anybody.

If anything you've just read strikes a chord with you and you want to know more, visit our *Steps to Salvation* section in the back of this book. Or find a friend who knows Jesus or a Bible-believing church in your area and talk to the pastor. As always, thanks for reading.

August 24, 2024
And That's the Truth

Quick, candidates aside, what's the one thing you dislike most about politics? As I think about this, we're in the home stretch of the presidential election. In fact, it's because of this that I began thinking about writing this post. I'm reminded of an entry in God's "big ten" of rules: "You shall not bear false witness." What does that mean? It's not only for application in a courtroom trial when you're on the stand. It's one of the guiding principles of life in general.

Anyone ever had their mouth washed out with soap because they lied? When my kids were growing up, they knew their punishment would always be worse if truth were a distant memory. They tried the other approach a couple times and soon learned that it wasn't worth it. It seems to me that our elected leaders could learn a thing or two from that same lesson. Could it be that the consequences of lying haven't been harsh enough to force a change in their behavior.

Paul Joseph Goebbels, Adolf Hitler's Propaganda Minister in Nazi Germany, said, "If you tell a lie often enough, it becomes the truth." Have you ever wondered why something that has been proven false continues to grow legs and be repeated over and over and over? It's the Goebbels principle. And it's successful because society has forgotten, through laziness or ignorance, how to discern truth from falsehood. We live in a sound-bite world.

I'm not absolving either political party, both are guilty. But it may be true that one side, aided by the media, has honed this practice to perfection. For example, what is the motivation for Congress to pass legislation that impacts most citizens and then exempts themselves? Hmm.

Where are today's truth seekers? Why has the world seemingly abandoned their responsibility to call out anything that doesn't line up with the truth? It's simple. Apart from the Bible, there is no absolute truth. Opinions reign supreme, and elite politicians believe their constituents are either asleep, too busy to pay attention, emotionally attached to the outcome of the lie--i.e. it benefits them, or they've heard it so often…it must be the truth. And you know what? They're right.

Remember as a kid when you used to follow the numbered dots with a pencil to discover the picture? We seem to have lost the ability to "connect the dots" in today's political arena. The following quote, generally attributed to Edmund Burke, but not original with him, contains much wisdom applicable to our current status: **The only thing necessary for the triumph of evil is that good men do nothing.**

How can we turn this barreling juggernaut around? Is there a way to return to civility in the midst of disagreements? Do you know the 2nd law of thermodynamics? Paraphrased it is: Everything in a closed system moves from order to chaos. The opposite is always true too: Nothing in a closed system moves from chaos to order.

The human condition, apart from a relationship with Jesus Christ, is on a slippery slope moving from order to chaos. I believe we're experiencing the birth pangs Jesus talked about in Matthew 24:7, 8, *"For nation will rise against nation, and kingdom against kingdom, and in various places there will be famines and earthquakes. But all these things are merely the beginning of birth pangs."*

Unfortunately, unlike a mother's pain that results in a new life, these birth pangs will usher in a period of unbelievable suffering and death…unless…

There is a pathway out of this, individually and corporately. But most people, individually or as a group, refuse to consider it. It's the pathway of freedom in the person of Jesus Christ. Jesus said, *"I am the way and the truth and the life, no one comes to the Father but through Me."* (John 14:6). The only possible way to avoid the coming judgment is to admit our sin and fall humbly on the grace of a loving God through His Son's death on a cross and resurrection from the grave.

This invitation is available to all. Jesus also said, *"the one who comes to Me I certainly will not cast out."* (John 6:37). This includes individuals of any race, color, creed or status…all who come on God's terms, will be welcomed. And, believe me, this is the truth you've been looking for, the truth you can base your eternal future on. Don't wait. Find a friend who knows Jesus or find a Bible-believing church and ask the pastor if this is true. Also, feel free to check out our *Steps to Salvation* pages in the back of this book.

September 28, 2024
Talk is Cheap

It's thirty-eight days before one of the most disrespectful elections I can re-member, and we are at the height of political rhetoric. Both sides seem to think bashing the opponent is more effective than civil discourse about the issues they would be elected to address. Badgering, bullying, and backbiting seem to be the primary criteria for speech writers. Sad.

The Bible has much to say about what comes out of our mouths. I under-stand there are many who don't embrace the Bible as any kind of authority. That too is sad. For where else can we find absolute truth? Pride and lying, kind of a one-two punch, top God's list of things He hates (Prov. 6:17). And you know the old joke about how do you tell that a politician is lying?

Here is just a sampling of God's thoughts on our speech:

"When there are many words, transgression is unavoidable, but he who restrains his lips is wise." Prov 10:19

"Let another praise you and not your own mouth." Prov. 27:2

"The mouth speaks out of that which fills the heart." Matt. 12:34

Do these verses offer insight into either or both of the main candidates? Can we draw valid conclusions about their character? What conclusions can be inferred about those of us who are one-trick ponies, a.k.a. one-issue voters who are not interested in reality, truth, or facts?

There is abundant anger and vitriol in the population because of the percep-tion that their candidate's opponent is a liar, a cheat, stupid, irrational, and many other descriptors to paint—in their own minds—the picture that their side has virtue, integrity, and truth in their corner. Both are wrong.

For those of us on the sidelines watching this melodrama unfold, we have the option to fret, wring our hands, and drink Pepto Bismal. Or we can trust the One who has everything under control and is allowing or orchestrating all things to "work together for good to those who love Him" (Rom. 8:28). God's plan, from eternity, is playing out in our lives in real time.

Prophecy is being fulfilled as we watch the world in turmoil. Is the end near? Nobody knows except God how or when the current Russia / Ukraine war will end. Nobody knows except God how current weather patterns play into His plan for the end of days. But what I do know, is that I want to be ready when He calls everybody out of the pool...and I am, because I know where I'll go when I die.

And if you don't already know where you'll spend eternity, you can. Today. The answer is in the same book where we learned what God thinks about our speech.

"He [God] says, 'At the acceptable time I listened to you, and on the day of salvation I helped you.' Behold, now is 'the acceptable time,' behold, now is 'the day of salvation.'" II Cor. 6:2

For the rest of the good news about your future, turn to the back of this book and read *Steps to Salvation*.

Thanks for reading.

October 9, 2024
God Said…So What?

Do you ever feel like, "so what"? God said, "let there be light, and there was." So what? God said, "it's gonna rain for 40 days", and it did. So what? God said, "It is finished". Do you see a pattern here? God says something—and something happens.

We talk about superpowers different from comic book characters, such as high intelligence, mechanical skills, patience with irritating people, etc. But there is nothing that says superpower like speaking something into existence. Anybody you know that can do that…besides God? So what?

The thing about God speaking is different than anyone on earth. He *cannot* lie (Tit. 1:2). So what? In life, we all want to make good decisions. How do we do that when, for example, politicians lie? We examine data, review history, seek counsel, and hope for the best with reasoning tainted by our environment and upbringing. So what?

I've just been reading through Revelation and I'm reminded of some of the things God said that are on the horizon. Ask yourself, "If God can't lie, how can I *not* consider seriously *everything* He says?"

Many have an opinion of God, assuming Him to be much like the ancient gods, angry unless appeased by human sacrifices or other aberrations of common sense. The Only true God is nothing like that. He speaks because He loves us and wants no mistakes in our thinking that would keep us from making the right choice. And what is that choice?

Jesus said, "I am the way and the truth and the life, no one comes to the Father but through Me" (John 14:6). If we don't assume this statement is true, why would we waste any time reading the Bible? We have become so skeptical in our present society, that we often don't stop to think that God *is not* like us and, as a result, come to wrong conclusions.

I've been asking "so what" throughout this post. It's time to answer that question. I assume you're reading this far because you want to make the right decision, a decision based on wisdom and truth. The answer to "so what" has eternal significance. If you make the wrong choice, you'll spend eternity in the last place you want to be, hell. There are only two destinations. Heaven and hell.

You say you don't believe in hell, and religion is for those who aren't smart enough, good-looking enough, or rich enough to accept a different way in life. The Bible says there are two ways and two gates, only two. One is wide. One is narrow. One leads to destruction with many entering there and the other leads to life and few find it (Matt. 7:13,14).

Why do you think that is? Are only a few smart enough or clever enough to follow the clues that lead to the treasure? No. But there are relatively few who are humble enough to believe everything God says and turn from their prideful, sinful ways to accept the free gift Jesus died on the cross to provide to any who come on His terms.

We've already seen that God *cannot* lie. This is the truth your future hangs on. If God didn't love you in spite of your poor prior choices, He wouldn't have said any of the things He has. The ball's in your court. Choose wisely.

Now you know the answer to "so what". What are you going to do about it? If you want to know more about what God thinks of you, go to the back of this book and read the section on *Steps to Salvation.*

Thanks for reading.

October 14, 2024
Give it up

"Give and it will be given to you...pressed down, shaken together and running over" (Luke 6:38a). We're in the run-up to a presidential election. Rarely does a day go by that I don't get one or more requests for support—read money—for this candidate or that proposition. Many of these are presented as surveys telling me how important my opinions are. That might be believable if they didn't all end with their pitch for a donation.

All non-profits run on donations. And it's not my goal to bash any of them. Many are legit and worth supporting. But those of us who follow Christ are required to be good stewards of that which He has entrusted to us. Due diligence suggests doing background checks before signing the checks. In the world of Christian giving, if an organization isn't vetted by the Evangelical Council for Financial Accountability (ECFA), you might want to dig a little deeper to be sure they're on the up and up.

Having said all this, the real question we should ask ourselves is, "Why should I give anything to anybody?" For believers in Jesus, the answer is simple: because God said to give. In Malachi 3:10, we're told "**Bring the whole tithe** into the storehouse, so that there may be food in my house, and **test Me** now in this" says the Lord of hosts, "if I will not open for you the windows of heaven and pour out for you a blessing until it overflows."

In Old Testament times, the tithe began at 10%. I'm not suggesting a legalistic approach to our giving. It's a heart matter between you and God. And God doesn't need our money. Giving is for our benefit. First, it proves our trust in God's ability and willingness to provide *our* needs. Second, it's a little like calling a bet in poker. This verse in Malachi is **the only place** in scripture where we're allowed to "test God." Jesus made that very clear when He rebuked Satan, "You shall not put the Lord your God to the test" (Matt. 4:7).

Many churches hesitate to talk about giving. Why? Is Jesus' command to "bring" any more or less demanding than, say, "love your neighbor"? What else do they *not* talk about because it may offend the hearers? When obedience is compromised, blessings are reduced or eliminated. Reread Malachi 3:10. Overflowing blessings are the result of obedience in this area. It's the computer programmer's IF-THEN statement.

I use the example of giving to shed light on a travesty of disobedience in the church today. Easily available statistics show the average churchgoer gives between 2% - 3% of their income; only 5% tithe and 80% give 2% or less.

The title of this post is: Give *it* up. What is 'it'? It's not more money. It keeps us from intimacy with our Father. It tops His list of "things I hate." Proverbs 6:17 in the NASB calls it "haughty eyes." Psalm 101:5b says, "…no one who has a haughty look and an arrogant heart will I endure." It causes us to think and act as if we could make it on our own, apart from God. It's the last thing many Christians want to deal with because it's so ingrained in our core we don't recognize it for what it is. It is the enemy of our very souls: Pride.

Failure to obey this command to give is just one result of sinful pride. It also indicates a preoccupation with self, a lack of compassion for others, but most of all, it indicates a small and ineffective faith in the One who sets the rules, provides our daily needs, and holds the keys to our future. Why is pride considered deadly? Because it lies to us and tells us "we're doing well, we don't need a Savior." Who do you think whispers that in our ears?

Humility is impossible when we think that all we have done and all that we are is strictly our own doing. But Paul reminds us, "What do you have that you did not receive, and if you did receive it, why do you boast as if you had not received it?" (I Cor. 4:7). Jesus told His disciples, "Freely you received, freely give" (Matt. 10:8).

The path back to an obedient relationship with the One who loves us enough to forgive even our pride, starts with recognizing how far we have drifted. Jesus said, "…the one who comes to Me I will certainly not cast out" (John 6:37). If you don't want to be cast into "outer darkness" (Matt.8:12; 22:13; 25:30), turn to Jesus before it's too late. Check out our *Steps to Salvation* in the back of this book for the path to your freedom from pride.

Thanks for reading.

Steps to Salvation

"He [God] says, 'At the acceptable time I listened to you, and on the day of salvation I helped you.' Behold, now is 'the acceptable time,' behold, now is 'the day of salvation.'" II Cor. 6:2

If you're reading this, I believe God is calling you to Himself. He wants a relationship with you to fellowship with you for eternity. There is no magic formula, no special words to recite, and no number of "things" you can do to bring about this relationship. **God has done it all** through His son, Jesus Christ.

The following steps are intended to help you understand your situation, from God's perspective, and open your eyes to the truth of Jesus' words, *"I am **the** way and **the** truth and **the** life, **no one** comes to the Father but through Me."* (Jn. 14:6) There is a sample prayer at the end that, if you are truly repentant, you can offer to God. The specific words aren't important; it's the humility in your heart that God looks at.

1.   There is a God. He is holy and hates sin. *"You shall be holy, for I am holy."* (I Peter 1:16.)

2.   Your sin separated you from God and deserves death.

*"For **all** have sinned and **fall short** of the glory of God"* (Rom. 3:23)

*"For **the wages of sin is death**, but the **free gift** of God is **eternal life** in Christ Jesus our Lord."* (Rom. 6:23.)

3.   God loves **you** so much He sent Jesus to earth to die **in your place**, to pay the penalty you could never pay on your own.

*"For God **so loved** the world that **He gave** His only begotten Son, that **whoever believes** in Him shall not perish, but have eternal life."* (Jn. 3:16)

4.   Good works, good attitudes, and good deeds **can't** solve your sin problem. You must believe that Jesus is THE **ONLY** WAY back to God, and trust that His death *on your behalf* erased *your* debt.

*"For **by grace** you have been **saved** through faith; and that **not of yourselves**, it is the **gift of God; not as a result of works**, so that no one may boast."* (Eph. 2:8,9.)

5.   Tell God you're sorry for your sin and you want to turn your life around.

*"...if you confess with your mouth Jesus as Lord, and believe in your heart that God raised Him from the dead, **you will be saved**;"* (Rom. 10:9.)

6.   Believe that you're forgiven and God restored you to fellowship with Him. *"Therefore there is now no condemnation for those who are in Christ Jesus."* (Rom. 8:1)

*"If we confess our sins, **He is faithful** and righteous **to forgive** us our sins and to cleanse us from **all** unrighteousness."* (I Jn. 1:9)

*"These things I have written to you who believe in the name of the Son of God, so   that **you may know** that **you have eternal life**."* (I Jn. 5:13)

The devil will try to tell you that nothing happened, that you're still the same worthless sinner you always were. Don't believe his lies. But you will know because you (and everybody else) will see a change in your attitudes, your desires, and you may even be drawn to different companions.

Jesus told a parable about a sower and four different results from the same seed. Only one of four took root and grew. Make sure you see the results of a changed life. If nothing changes and lasts, come back to this list, and examine yourself to see if it was real. Read the whole story about the Sower and seeds in Luke 8:4-8.

7.   Tell everyone what has just happened to you.

You Believe in Jesus Christ as your Savior; You are a child of God; Your sins are forgiven; Your relationship with God has been restored Your eternity in Heaven is guaranteed

8.   Find a **Bible-believing** church and **become involved** with fellowship and service. Ask the pastor about believer's baptism and plan for this outward display of the inward change that has taken place.

9.   Spend time daily reading the Bible and talking to God (prayer).

Lord God, I confess that I am a sinner and my sin has separated me from You, and there's nothing I can do on my own to change that. I believe that Jesus came to earth and died on the cross for my sin, rose again on the 3rd day, and that He is the only way back to You. I want to receive Your free gift of salvation in Jesus. Thank You for hearing my prayer. **Amen.**

About the Author

Mike Thornton

Mike Thornton grew up in Southern California. He served as an Army drill sergeant during Vietnam. After a downhill slide, he surrendered his life to Jesus Christ.

Mike spent over three decades in the communications industry and sold and managed sales and operations for high-tech companies. He also sold oil investments for 8 years. He is the author of *Christ in Men...Today*, a 52-week men's devotional building spiritual muscle one character quality at a time and *Beyond the MBA to an MBB*, a must-read for those in Customer Service.

He is a private pilot, and he and Linda, his wife of 53 years, met at Bible School in California, live in Colorado Springs, and have 4 children (2 already in Heaven), 8 grandchildren and one great-grandson.

www.ingramcontent.com/pod-product-compliance
Lightning Source LLC
Chambersburg PA
CBHW062128020426

42335CB00013B/1140